A COWBOY CHRISTMAS

A COWBOY CHRISTMAS

Western Celebrations, Recipes, and Traditions

SHANNA HATFIELD

TWODOT

GUILFORD, CONNECTICUT
HELENA, MONTANA

A · TWODOT® · BOOK

An imprint and registered trademark of The Rowman & Littlefield
Publishing Group, Inc.
4501 Forbes Blvd., Ste. 200
Lanham, MD 20706
www.rowman.com

Distributed by NATIONAL BOOK NETWORK

British Library Cataloguing in Publication Information available

Library of Congress Cataloging-in-Publication Data

Names: Hatfield, Shanna, author.
Title: A cowboy Christmas : Western celebrations, recipes, and
    traditions / Shanna Hatfield.
Description: Helena, Montana : TwoDot, [2019] | Includes index. |
Identifiers: LCCN 2019014738 (print) | LCCN 2019019087 (ebook) |
    ISBN 9781493042357 (e-book) | ISBN 9781493042340 (hardback :
    alk. paper)
Subjects: LCSH: Christmas cooking. | Christmas decorations. | Hatfield,
    Shanna, 1971- —Friends and associates. | LCGFT: Cookbooks.
Classification: LCC TX739.2.C45 (ebook) | LCC TX739.2.C45 H37 2019
    (print) | DDC 641.5/686—dc23
LC record available at https://lccn.loc.gov/2019014738

♾™ The paper used in this publication meets the minimum
requirements of American National Standard for Information
Sciences—Permanence of Paper for Printed Library Materials, ANSI/
NISO Z39.48-1992.

I dedicate this book to three very special people:
To Mom and Dad for giving me a love of the
holidays, showing me the joys of opening my
heart and home to others, and providing me with
rural roots that run deep.
To my husband for his love, support, and always
being there for me. You are amazing, and I
am grateful every day for the blessing of being
married to you.

CONTENTS

ACKNOWLEDGMENTS

A project like this book would have been impossible to begin—let alone finish—without the help of some wonderful, generous people.

With a bounty of gratitude, I extend my thanks to the fabulous families who allowed me to interview them and share their stories as well as family recipes: Justin and Tona Andrade, Shana and Justin Bailey, Casey and Kacee Colletti, Amy and Jim Fenley, John and Carla Harrison, Nick and Megan LaDuke, Sue McKinnon, Derek and Jessica Miller, Hank and Renee Moss, and Tate and Kristin Stratton.

I also am so thankful to Erin Turner and the folks at Globe Pequot/TwoDot Books for providing the opportunity to create this book. Erin has been absolutely incredible, and I'm so glad I had the privilege of working with her. Her encouragement and professionalism are unparalleled and made the process go so smoothly. It's a dream come true to do this book that combines three of my favorite things in the world: Christmas, cowboys, and cooking!

Friends and family shared ideas for decorations, recipes, and people to contact who might be interested in being included in the book. I'm especially thankful to Julie Jutten for putting me in touch with the rodeo families featured here. My thanks also go to the good people at the Justin Cowboy Crisis Fund for their help.

And I can't forget to thank my niece, Jessie Friend, who spent hours and hours helping me decorate sugar cookies. She is a trouper!

Finally, my gratitude goes out to my husband, Captain Cavedweller, who put up with months of craziness while I worked on the book along with various other writing projects. He didn't even blink when I asked him to dig Christmas decorations out of the barn in the midst of an August heat wave, or when he came home to find Christmas cookies covering every surface in the kitchen. As I cooked my way through every single recipe included in this book, he good-naturedly tried each one. When I was running close to deadlines, he took over cooking our meals and offered help whenever and wherever he could. I am so blessed by and thankful for his ongoing support and encouragement.

CHRISTMAS WITH A COUNTRY GIRL

WHEN THE OPPORTUNITY POPPED UP TO DO THIS BOOK, I was beyond excited. It combines a variety of things I'm passionate about: Christmas, country life, and cooking.

A love of all three of these things was cultivated during my childhood. My growing-up years were spent on a farm in eastern Oregon where my family waged battle against sagebrush, rocks, and the random juniper tree to till the soil for crops and plant pasture grass. It wasn't until I found myself far away from home, living in a big city, that I realized how fortunate I was to have a foundation with country roots on which to build my future.

The only thing my dad ever wanted to be was a farmer. During the first dozen years of my parents' marriage, he worked for a variety of farmers and ranchers while they saved every penny they could. In the early 1960s, they purchased the farm where they would reside in a small but close-knit community for the next fifty years.

Twenty years into their marriage, with three teenagers in the house, the last thing my parents expected was to discover they were expecting. My formative years were spent running wild and free on the farm where dad raised hay, wheat, corn, and cattle. My childhood brimmed with sunshine, hay fever, and a never-ending supply of rural learning experiences.

With my two brothers and their families living nearby, an ample supply of adults kept their eye on me—even if their vigilant supervision didn't necessarily keep me out of trouble. I always had horses to ride, fences to climb, and an adventure waiting around the corner. My love for cowboys and the western way of life came naturally.

My oldest brother worked as a ranch hand on remote ranches and would come home after weeks (sometimes what seemed like months) away, brimming with hair-raising tales that spurred my interest and imagination. Sometimes, he'd bring along a fellow cowpoke in need of a home-cooked meal and a few days of rest before they headed back to the ranch. I'd sit in rapt adoration, listening to them talk about a way of life that seemed to be all but disappearing. And they brought with them the fragrances of leather and horses and sage-soaked sunshine—a scent I still love to this day.

The cowboys my brother brought home to visit were just a few of the many guests who pulled up a chair at our dinner table over the years.

My parents both come from big families who love to get together for the holidays. Since our house could accommodate large gatherings, we hosted many Christmas celebrations for extended family.

If we had snow, Dad would take down part of the fence around the pasture right behind our house so we could speed down the hill on tractor inner tubes and toboggans. My Christmas vacations were full of sledding, ice skating on the pond, snowmobiling, and attempting to build snow forts on the front lawn.

During our holiday celebrations, I learned so much about entertaining from my parents. Over the years, I've participated in and attended more big family gatherings than I can count. Not only did my parents set a good entertaining example, but that theme of making guests feel welcome carried over to the homes of my aunts and uncles and grandparents, who also took turns hosting our noisy, boisterous bunch.

My mother taught me how to feed a crowd, prepare in advance, and make food stretch when necessary. She could turn the most basic ingredients into delicious dishes with a grandkid or two underfoot while visiting with guests. From watching my grandmothers, aunts, and mother pour their love into their cooking, I learned to do the same.

Our home was festive and welcoming to everyone who walked through the door. Guests would be plied with homemade candies and cookies and invited to warm up by the fire.

What I know about being a gracious host came from my Dad. I don't think he's ever met anyone he wouldn't invite to stay for dinner, and he's a master at making people feel welcome.

Christmas has always been such a special time for him because it's also his birthday. I have so many wonderful memories of early Christmas mornings because of Daddy's joyful enthusiasm to greet the day. He passed that love of the holiday to me along with the delight it brings when we gather with those we care about most.

And amid the flurry of wrapping paper and preparations for a house full of guests remained the true reason for the season.

Christmas was such a magical, wondrous, positively amazing time of year when I was a child, and is no doubt the reason I adore the holiday today. In fact, I love Christmas so much that my husband, Captain Cavedweller, and I wed just a week before Christmas twenty-five years ago.

My love for the holidays, the country way of life, and cooking from the heart is why I'm so excited to share this book with you.

In the following pages, you'll find stories with rodeo and rural families who talk about some of their favorite Christmas memories and traditions. Glean ideas to help you relax and streamline the entertaining process through the holidays. Learn a few gift-wrapping tips or gather ideas for hostess gifts. And be ready to try a collection of recipes that may become new family favorites!

I hope you enjoy this book written with love and shared with all the joy of this beautiful holiday season!

Merry Christmas from our home and hearts to yours!

—*Shanna Hatfield*

PART ONE

CELEBRATE THE COWBOY WAY

DECK THE HALLS

DURING MY GROWING-UP YEARS, MY PARENTS had plenty of room for company at our home and a sledding hill with a pond for skating right outside the back door. We almost always hosted Christmas at our house for one side of the family or the other, with sometimes as many as fifty guests in attendance. It was during these festive gatherings that I learned many lessons from my parents about entertaining with grace and ease.

A gathering is more than just an opportunity to break bread together. It's an opportunity to connect lives, deepen friendships, and share in the wonder of the Christmas.

Meet a couple from Oklahoma who know all about entertaining and making folks feel right at home. Then learn tips for making entertaining at home a snap as you open your doors and deck your halls this holiday season.

TATE AND KRISTIN STRATTON

HOW DOES A BULL-RIDING, BOOT-SELLING COWBOY CELEBRATE CHRISTMAS?

By baking pies, of course.

Rodeo cowboy Tate Stratton proudly carries on a tradition started by his father of making pies for the holidays.

"My dad was an entertainer and loved to host parties or gatherings. Dad was the one volunteering to host events at our house," Tate said. "We had pecan and pumpkin pie when I was a kid at a big get-together. I remember Dad sent home pies with our guests. Now, I make pumpkin and pecan pies. There's nothing easier than a pecan pie."

Tate loves to cook, and his wife, Kristin, enjoys baking, too. But this couple from Bristow, Oklahoma, really loves to entertain.

"The joy of the family and the blessings they bring are so much a part of the season," Tate said.

Their friendly natures are the reason Tate and Kristin happened to meet through Tate's rodeo traveling partner. Tate was traveling across Kansas in 2008, and his friend's cell phone kept going off in the middle of the night. He finally picked up the phone and texted back the caller, who just happened to be Kristin. She was traveling home from West Virginia with her parents and awake on the long drive. Throughout the night, they exchanged text messages. They ended up meeting for lunch and, according to Tate, the "rest is history."

The couple wed May 14, 2010, and made a home in Kellyville, Oklahoma, near Kristin's parents. "I've only moved twice in my life. Once, next door to my parents, and then to where we live now. Tate likes to tell me I'm sheltered," Kristin said with a laugh. "I say it is just stability. I've seen a lot of the country thanks to rodeo and a job I used to have. I'm not sheltered at all, actually, but home is home. There's nothing like going home to me. It's a safe place that's warm and cozy."

While Kristin has deep roots in Oklahoma, Tate was born in Oklahoma but raised in Stanley, New Mexico. His parents had eighty acres of flatland where they ran cattle and horses.

"We always had horses, show horses—Appaloosas," Tate said.

Rodeo caught his interest from a young age.

"I loved to watch it. When I was eight, I decided I wanted to participate in an Easter rodeo by riding a calf. Dad brought home two calves and turned them loose in a round pen. I got in there with a neighbor boy and climbed on the bigger of the two. The other one was a little wiry, and the neighbor kid ate dirt riding it. But I was hooked."

After that first rodeo, Tate went on to compete through middle school and high school. After graduating from high school, he attended Western Texas College in Snyder. It was during his

courtesy of Tate Stratton

first year of college that he won the College National Finals Rodeo and was crowned College World Champion. He graduated at the top of his class then transferred to Texas A&M University where he graduated with a Bachelor of Science degree in animal science.

He moved to Oklahoma and qualified for his first Wrangler National Finals Rodeo (WFNR) in 2009, but injuries kept him sidelined the following year.

"During a ride in Reno, I jammed my wrist. I battled with a hand injury for months, trying to figure out what was going on," Tate said.

He ended up seeing a specialist in Dallas, Texas, and had surgery. He couldn't compete for a while and didn't want to reach out for help, but eventually sent an email to the Justin Cowboy Crisis Fund.

"The funds the JCCF gave us helped us get back on our feet," Tate said. "It was a hand up, not a hand out. It just goes against our nature to ask for help, but sometimes we need it. The [Justin] Sportsmedicine Team® keeps us on the road, and the JCCF helps get us back on the road. It's amazing to see how willing people are to get on board to support the JCCF."

Tate came back strong in 2011 and qualified once again for the WNFR, and made his third qualification in 2012.

He continued on the rodeo road, with Kristin going along when she could.

Then, in January 2015, life changed when their daughter Merritt was born. Daughter Henley joined the family in December 2017.

"I was thinking about 'how can I get home' rather than 'how can I get on the road' after my daughter was born," Tate said. "It's feast or famine in rodeo, and when Merritt came into the picture, things changed."

The stress of worrying about where the paychecks were coming from and how he could provide for his family outweighed his love of riding.

Chippewa, a division of the Justin Boots brand, was in need of a territory manager and Tate took the job. From there he's moved up to territory manager at Justin Boots, overseeing the Kansas, Oklahoma, Arkansas, and Missouri territories.

"I don't want to be a typical sales rep. I want to be me. I'm not there to sell something, but to help meet a need," Tate said.

He also has been helping to meet the needs of young up-and-coming cowboys through Professional Rodeo Cowboys Association youth rodeos.

"It was a natural fit to work with kids, and I have no problem talking in front of people. The outreach worked well, and when they saw how I handled it, they started calling on me more," Tate said. "I'm very blessed to have the career that I did, but now I can give back to the next generation."

Both Kristin and Tate put family at the top of their list of joys for the holidays. One of their favorite things about Christmas is "the family time, getting everyone together," Tate said. "The food is awesome. We break bread together and enjoy having our family together."

The gift of love sprinkled into the meals served at their home is something Tate learned from his father.

"There were special dishes that were only fixed during the holidays, and I looked forward to them. Dad loved to cook. Just thinking about how much money our family spent on food during the holidays, when funds were limited, shows how much the holidays meant to him because he would spend days cooking."

Memories of those special times with his father and how he shared his love through cooking inspire Tate and Kristin to do the same.

"I love opening my home up to anyone and everyone," Kristin said. "I want our home to be a place for community. For anyone to feel welcomed and loved."

And if visitors are lucky, they'll leave with one of Tate's pecan or pumpkin pies, baked from the heart and sent home with love.

ENTERTAINING AT HOME FOR THE HOLIDAYS

SO MANY PEOPLE HAVE A PRECONCEIVED IDEA about entertaining at home. Some think it is an involved and much-to-be-avoided process. If you are one of those, let's shift the way you view entertaining.

In its most basic form, entertaining at home is opening your doors and making others feel welcome. It isn't about how well you cook or if your home appears magazine-worthy.

Entertaining at home *is* all about the way your guests feel when they head out your door.

Did you create fun or warm memories? Did you focus on enjoying the time spent together? Were you present in the moment, interacting with your guests?

A warm and gracious host is the one who views entertaining at home as an opportunity to share, to welcome guests and make them feel like they are the most important people in the world right at that moment. When guests feel truly welcomed and appreciated, the dust bunnies beneath the fridge and the fingerprints on the patio door won't matter at all.

Give yourself a measure of grace, find a new entertaining standard, and have some fun. Put your guests at ease, make them feel special, and see how much easier entertaining becomes.

When you are planning to welcome more than a few guests, these secrets to entertaining will give you the foundation you need to entertain with ease and look like a pro.

PLEASE JOIN US FOR A

Christmas Party

SATURDAY, DECEMBER 21ST

6 P.M.

The Claus Home

123 REINDEER LANE, NORTH POLE

RSVP

NICK AT 555-555-1234

PICK A THEME

Selecting a theme for your gathering simplifies the entertaining process by narrowing menu selections, providing decorating ideas and color schemes, and making it so much more fun to entertain.

Of course Christmas is its own wonderful theme, but you can play off that in many different ways. Traditional, whimsical, and modern are just a few of the twists you can put on a Christmas theme.

Here are a few ideas for holiday themed parties:

An Ornament Exchange: Invite everyone to bring one gift-wrapped ornament. Specify a price range. As guests arrive, put a number on each package and a corresponding number in a bowl or hat. After dessert, have everyone draw a number and open the corresponding gift.

Sledding or Skating Party: You don't have to be a child to enjoy an afternoon of sledding or skating with friends. When the fun is over, troop back inside to thaw out with a spread of light appetizers and sweets, served buffet style. Don't forget to have plenty of warm beverages to sip!

Cookie or Candy Exchange: If you don't have time to bake a dozen different types of treats, make one huge batch and invite your friends to do the same. Invite them over for an afternoon of swapping treats, making sure they bring enough for party attendees to each take home a dozen. Serve a few savory snacks and, of course, something to sip!

Card-Writing Party: Mix holiday business with pleasure by hosting an evening gathering with a few close friends to write Christmas cards. Tell your guests to bring their cards, envelopes, address books, pens, and stamps. You'll provide background music, space at a table, and an outstanding dessert or two for motivation.

Trimming the Tree Party: Change the look of your tree from past years by asking others to help you deck the halls. Invite a few friends over and let creativity be the guide. Play your favorite Christmas music and offer hearty soup, sandwiches, and sweet treats as the reward for their efforts.

MAKE A PLAN

Decide what you want your party or event to look like. Where will you host it and when? Who will you invite? Think of it as the four Ws:

What: Do you want a sit-down dinner for six or a buffet for twenty? Formal or casual? Indoors or outdoors?

When: If you work weekdays, a weekend event might be a better option. If you are a morning person, make it a brunch gathering. A night owl should focus on a late evening party. Hold the party when your energy level is highest.

Where: Location helps to define the mood and spirit of a party. Think beyond the traditional dining room event. Try the den for a night of family games or the sunroom for a morning get-together. The center island of your kitchen is a great spot for informal dining. Build a buffet on top.

Who: Who do you want to attend your party? Is it a family affair? All adults or are kids invited? A girls' night out? A gathering of friends? Neighbors? People from work? Think about creating a good mix of people who will mingle and enjoy one another.

SPECIAL TOUCHES

Spend a little time on the extras that give your party a "Wow" factor by engaging your guests' senses.

The sense of smell is very important and one of the first things guests notice when they walk into your home. Create a comforting aroma. Just as colors and sounds trigger emotional responses, smells have wonderful—or not so wonderful—effects on our mood. Your guests' initial impression of a party may not be what first hits their eyes and ears, but their nose. Choose one scent and stick with it throughout your home. Make sure to include the fragrance in the guest bathroom, too.

Perfect party lighting is also important. Parties are a good time to let the shadows fall where they may. Rely on lights from decorations, strategically placed candles, and a few soft lights. You don't want your

home to be dark, but softly and warmly lit. If you have a fireplace, make sure it is going because the light is inviting and marvelous. Create a cozy atmosphere where your guests want to linger. Substitute lower-wattage lightbulbs during your parties or hit the dimmer switch. It makes an amazing difference to the ambience.

Background music adds a lovely touch to a party. For a big gathering of mixed ages, choose mellow tunes. If your party has a high energy vibe, go for upbeat music.

You can even add special little touches when you set the table, like a small gift for each guest or a sprig of greenery that accents the plate.

Try to engage all the senses for a memorable experience.

HELPFUL TIPS FOR YOUR HOLIDAY HOME

Most of us have the best of intentions to have a sparkling clean house when we entertain. But if it is the night before the big event and things are looking chaotic, don't panic. Attention to a few specific areas will give the appearance of a neat, orderly home.

Entry: Make sure the outside of your door is clutter and dirt free. Check the interior entry area and repeat the decluttering process. Light a candle and add a holiday floral arrangement in this area to create a welcoming atmosphere as guests enter your home. Put down a mat both inside and outside the front door to help keep floors clean.

Kitchen: The kitchen truly is the heart of the home and where most people tend to gather. Clean the floors, clear off the counters, and wipe down surfaces. Give the fridge a quick wipe-down inside and out, and polish the sink's faucet. Set out a few decorations and have something for early arrivers to do while they wait for the party to get started. Involved guests are more likely to mingle, which adds to the fun. You could have them roll silverware in napkins, chop salad ingredients, arrange serving platters—anything they are comfortable doing.

Bathroom: Of all the rooms to clean fanatically, this is the one. Scrub everything, take out the garbage, and make sure faucets and mirrors are shiny. Add flowers and a candle or fragrance plug-in in this area. If the bathroom is clean and sparkling, it is likely no one will notice anything amiss in the rest of the house. Make absolutely sure there are extra hand towels, as well as plenty of soap, facial tissues, and toilet paper available. Although you hate to think of it, also have a plunger available for a guest to use if necessary.

Gathering Room: In whatever room you are planning to set your buffet or eat the meal, spend a bit of time dusting, polishing, cleaning floors, and creating a warm atmosphere with lighting, candles, and music. Remember, candlelight or dimmed lights hide a multitude of imperfections!

Coat Closet: If you have a coat closet, clean it out completely before the party. Make sure it is stocked with plenty of sturdy hangers. Enlist an older child or neighborhood teen to serve as a coat checker. Make sure he or she understands the duties before the guests arrive.

HOLIDAY FLORALS

Flower arrangements and fresh greens add a wonderful, welcoming touch to your home. Holiday florals don't need to be expensive to make a visual impact. Even trimmings from your Christmas tree can be tucked into a container and used as a centerpiece. Add a jar with fairy lights and a few pinecones for a festive addition to your holiday table!

With any type of centerpiece that will be around food, steer away from highly scented florals. They can overpower the food aromas, and some guests may be bothered by strong scents. Also, choose florals

that don't "shed." The last thing you want is a trail of little green fronds floating into your food.

Mirrored trays and candles are nice accents for your centerpiece and create a beautifully finished look.

When you make an arrangement, use an odd number of stems, especially if it is a small grouping. Flowers should be about one and a half times as tall as your container.

Keep your flowers in water—whether purchased from a store or cut fresh outside your home. Each time you expose floral stems to air, be sure to recut the stems on an angle under lukewarm water. If you will be storing the flowers before making the arrangement, put them somewhere cool and dark in a clean bucket with lukewarm water.

Crisscross floral tape (found at craft stores) over the top of your container to create a frame for your flowers. Add plenty of greenery or fillers to the arrangement to hide the tape.

You can also use floral foam to keep your stems upright and in place. Floral foam (again, look at a craft store) should be soaked in water until there are no air bubbles and then placed in the container. Trim the foam with a serrated knife, leaving about one inch above your container. Use the trimmed-off pieces to stuff down the sides of the container, filling in gaps to hold the foam securely in place. If it still feels wobbly, use floral tape across the top of the container to anchor the foam. Arrange your flowers and greenery in the foam, making sure you stick some in the sides and all around the top to conceal the foam.

Poinsettias make lovely centerpieces. Tuck them into a container that reflects your personality.

When purchasing a poinsettia, pull back the foil that is wrapped around the pot and check to make sure the leaves aren't turning yellow or falling off. The plant should have lots of colored leaves (bracts) with the small yellow flowers in the center intact or just beginning to open. Keep poinsettias in a sunny location away from drafts or heat, and keep soil moist but not wet.

Have fun with your flowers; they not only add a welcome touch of color to your home, but are also a reflection of your personality!

HOLIDAY BUFFET

One of my favorite things about entertaining is presentation—making things look pretty. There is something so fun about deciding what serving pieces to use, what looks good where, and then having the whole thing come together just before the doorbell rings.

When you are planning to entertain, think about serving the food buffet style. This method of serving does two wonderful things:

- It keeps the host from being tied to the food and the kitchen.

- It creates a casual atmosphere where guests feel at ease and are more likely to mingle.

Don't you love it when your guests are hanging out and chatting? Kinda the whole point of entertaining.

Buffets can be set up in advance. Get creative and let your personal style shine through.

Step 1: Position your table where you'd like to set up your buffet. If you want people to move on both sides, make sure there is plenty of room for them to walk all the way around it. For a one-sided buffet, push your table against the wall to maximize creativity and height.

Step 2: Drape your table with a neutral cloth. White and cream look nice, but I like black best. It makes the colors of your serving pieces and food pop while hiding spills. If you can't find a tablecloth in your preferred color, flat sheets are an inexpensive alternative.

Step 3: Add height to your table to amp up the visual appeal. Focus the tallest point off-center and create a bit of a "waterfall" effect. Place the highest point at the back and off to one side, then decrease the height as you come forward and toward the other side. Height can come from a variety of items like sturdy boxes, stacks of books, even cooking pots turned upside down. Just be mindful of what you are setting where. You wouldn't place a huge platter on a small box, for example. If you have serving stands, these are also fabulous to use to give both height and texture to your table.

Step 4: Drape the elements you used to provide height with a matching cloth, then add another colorful cloth for an accent. Don't worry about making it perfectly smooth. It won't be. Embrace the lumps and wrinkles and give them a bit of a fluff to look artistic.

Step 5: Position all your serving pieces, tweak them to perfection, and leave them there until you are ready to fill them with food. If there is a possibility you will forget what food item goes in which serving dish, label them with sticky notes. Set up the table a few days ahead of your party and save yourself oodles of time the day your company arrives.

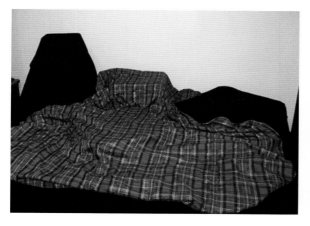

OH, WHAT FUN!

LIKE THE CLASSIC CHRISTMAS CAROL CLAIMS, it is such fun to go on a sleigh or horse ride in the winter. We've gone on a few over the years, and each experience has made a wonderful holiday memory.

There's just nothing like being tucked beneath a blanket on a nippy December day with the cold stinging your nose and cheeks while you ride along, taking life at a much slower pace, even if only for a short while.

One southeastern Washington couple makes it a point to help create memorable experiences through the carriage rides they offer on Christmas Eve.

Read about their holiday traditions and discover tips for outdoor winter fun!

courtesy of Amy Fenley

AMY AND JIM FENLEY

O N CHRISTMAS EVE, WHEN MOST PEOPLE are rushing around preparing for holiday gatherings, church services, and the arrival of St. Nicholas, one Prescott, Washington, couple is bringing holiday cheer to others.

Amy and Jim Fenley take people on carriage rides around historic downtown Walla Walla.

"It's a lot of fun to share the service we offer with people. Some couples and families have made this their Christmas Eve tradition, coming for a ride every year," Amy said. "One year, it was only nineteen degrees outside, and of all the reservations we had, only one canceled."

The rides they give Christmas Eve are by reservation only, although the couple does thirty-minute historic home tours every weekend from March through December with no reservations required.

Years ago, the couple had been working on a business plan to start a carriage business in the area. With a vibrant wedding industry and a beautiful downtown full of historic buildings and homes in Walla Walla, they saw a business opportunity.

courtesy of Kevin Peck

"We thought it would be a great area to do carriage rides," Amy said of Walla Walla, a town that was voted "Friendliest Small Town in America" by Rand McNally's Best of the Road contest in 2011. "We started looking for a horse, thinking we'd get into business with just one."

Just across the border in Oregon, Jim and Amy happened upon a dapple gray Percheron gelding named Maddock. The horse had been part of a team, but the team was split up because Maddock was half a hand too short for someone who was searching for eighteen-hand horses.

"We were offered a package deal for Maddock, the carriage, and harness," Amy said. The carriage was high quality, and the offer was one they couldn't pass up.

Amy and Jim have both worked around horses all their lives. When he was a boy, Jim and his two brothers trained horses, riding as many as five to six a day. At that time, he was living in a small community near Seattle. A surge of people wanted to get out of town and were buying "farmettes." Many hadn't been around animals, but sought out trained horses.

Amy was raised on a farm with her three sisters in Moscow, Idaho, and has always loved both Christmas and horses. She and Jim met when they were employed at a car dealership there.

"I worked in the office and Jim sold cars," Amy said.

Friendly interest grew into something more, and they began dating. The couple wed in June 2005 and made the move to the Walla Walla Valley.

"We love it here," Amy said. "The little communities here are wonderful, and we have great neighbors."

Through their carriage business, they've learned many details about the area's history, particularly the places on their historic homes tour.

"Maddock doesn't really need us, because he knows the route," Amy said with a laugh. "He knows which houses to stop at so Jim can provide the history, and he'll notice if things change at one of the houses."

Since their carriage business was going well, Jim bought a wagon that needed refurbished.

When it was ready for use, the couple purchased a team of black Percheron/Shire crosses from Ron Colton, who has his own carriage business in Baker City, Oregon. From the same sire, the two horses were born the same year and have always been together. If one has to go to the vet, both get loaded into the trailer.

Ned and Jed are showy additions who pull a large wagon the Fenleys use for festivals, events, and private rentals.

"They have a lot of go," Jim said of Ned and Jed. "When we first got them, we tried to weigh down the wagon with hay so they'd have a harder time pulling, but it just made them work harder and didn't slow them down."

With the wagon and carriage, the couple have worked a variety of weddings, anniversaries, birthday celebrations, proposals, family reunions, corporate events, rides at schools, and parades.

Ned and Jed pull the couple's vis-à-vis carriage in the Westward Ho Parade during the annual Pendleton Round-Up Rodeo.

"We're hired by the board to drive royalty in the parade and it's so fun," Amy said. "We just love it."

Some of the most memorable and emotional services they've provided is pulling a hearse owned by one of the local mortuaries.

"Once, we drove the hearse for a funeral for a young military veteran. To be part of that was such an honor," Jim said.

"And so emotional," Amy added.

courtesy of Kailee Meyer Photography

For the most part, though, AJ Carriages is all about having a good time. Their business catch-phrase is "the most fun you'll ever have at three miles an hour!"

While they enjoy the business and the people they meet, the holidays are Amy's favorite time of year.

"I love Christmas!" she said with a smile. Since she is 100 percent Norwegian, Amy grew up with a variety of traditions. "Christmas has always been a big deal in my family. It was my mom's favorite time of year. She'd go over the top with decorations and baking."

Many of those decorations now fill Amy's home. She loves the traditions and cherished treasures that have been handed down through generations.

"Christmas is about getting family together. A Norwegian tradition is to have a big family meal on Christmas Eve and then we open gifts. On Christmas Day, when I was growing up, we often had friends over for a meal who had nowhere else to celebrate the day."

The Fenleys know about giving gifts to others, too. They've done wagon rides for churches while they go caroling.

And then there are the carriage rides they offer on Christmas Eve.

"We want to share our holidays, share something we enjoy with others," Jim said.

Amy agreed. "The carriage rides on Christmas Eve are fun, and we're happy to share that with others, to become part of their traditions."

ROUGH STOCK RIDER

By Jim Fenley

They're a different breed these rough stock riders,
    You'd swear they were crazy if you weren't an insider.
For it's the thrill, the challenge they seek,
    It's an adrenaline rush, not for the meek.
I met one at the round up, back of the chutes,
    Younger than the rest, new chaps, hat and boots.
A determined young man tho, you could tell by his strut.
    He just knew he could ride anything that could buck.
I've seen rough stock riders, they come and they go
    Most never cut it, not past the first go.
But this young cowboy, I'm not sure why,
    I just knew he was different, I could tell he had try.
He climbed up on the chute, and I did, too.
    'Cuz I wanted to see just what he would do,
When he looked into the chute at that big wooly beast,
    Would he show fear in his eyes or hesitate in the least.
But no, he just climbed right on with a grin
    You'd think that his blood was ice water thin.
He eased down on his mount, adjusted his gear.
    The bullfighter shoutin' advice I was sure he couldn't hear.
'Cuz it's about that time that the adrenaline rush
    Fills up a cowboy 'til he'll swear he could bust.
It blurs out the world 'til there's nothin' to see,
    'Cept the shoulders and head of the beast 'tween his knees.
This is the rush, the legal high,
    That focuses a cowboy on himself and his ride.
With a nod of his head and one arm held high,
    He busts past the gate, the announcer yells "OUTSIDE!"
The ride, just six seconds beginning to end, but during
    That time he can't hear the fans.
        His world is the sheep strapped to his hand.
Just a sheep to the crowd, and a cute "mutton buster"
    But he rode with determination,
       and all the strength he could muster.
With adrenaline flowing he still didn't hear,
    His ride was over, 'til the bullfighter came near.
Said "good ride kid" and then with a jerk
    Pulled him off his sheep and set him down in the dirt.
The stands went wild and stood up to cheer
    He gave a two-handed wave, threw his hat in the air.
Hedeman, Frost, Murray, nor Gay,
    Had any more try than that cowboy that day.

LET IT SNOW

FEW WERE THE WINTERS DURING MY CHILDHOOD YEARS when we didn't have snow. I remember one year we'd planned a surprise birthday party for my dad (who was born on Christmas Day) with all his family coming to celebrate. We'd had snow earlier in December, but much of it had melted. The hill where we always went sledding behind our house caught the morning sun and most of the snow was gone before Christmas Eve rolled around. A loud noise behind the house drew Mom and me to the window. There was Dad in the loader tractor, dumping bucket after bucket of snow on the sled run so we could play on Christmas Day. That's when we realized the party was no longer a surprise, but we had a great time anyway!

Some of my most wonderful winter memories come from time spent sledding, skating, and building snow forts and snowmen.

Did you know there are tips that can help you build a better snowman? Or that a tin can along with a nail and a hammer can give you a glorious light to set outside on a winter night?

It's true!

Grab your scarf and mittens and prepare for some outdoor Christmas fun!

WELCOMING ENTRY

HAVE FUN DECORATING THE OUTSIDE OF YOUR HOME as well as the inside for Christmas. It's wonderful to spread a little cheer that greets guests who arrive at your door through some simple decorations.

When decorating a porch or exterior entry area, you don't have to spend oodles of money to make it a lovely, welcoming, cheerful space.

A few ideas to decorate it include:

- **Lights**—Christmas lights strung along eaves, wrapped around porch posts, and draped over doorways make a strong holiday welcome statement. Today there are many lighting choices including flickering snowflake lights, LED curtain lights, and icicle lights actually shaped like icicles.

- **Greenery**—Use clippings left over from wrangling your tree into the tree stand or ask for extras when you buy a tree. You can also purchase branches at a variety of stores in December. Place greenery in baskets, pots, galvanized buckets, or my favorite—milk cans. Use pine garlands, swags, and mini trees for adding to that wintry feel.

- **Natural Elements**—Add pinecones, red berries, twigs, or fun-shaped branches (like curly willow) to accent your greenery.

- **Vintage Treasures**—Drape a pair of old ice skates over a long-forgotten wooden sled and prop it near your front door for a big focal point as guests ring the doorbell. Wooden skis, apple baskets, worn-out boots, frayed rope, and old lanterns all make great props for creating nostalgic appeal around your front door.

EXTERIOR ILLUMINATION

The phrase "exterior illumination" always makes me smile and think of a Griswold family Christmas. You don't have to get all crazy to have beautiful lights outside your home. In fact, it's easy to hang just a string of lights or two that will add a bit of cheer to dark winter evenings.

If you plan to illuminate the outside of your home with holiday lights, here are some tips to help streamline the process:

- **Grab Your Gear**—Set up your ladder. Make sure it's safe, sturdy, and will reach the highest point you plan to light.

- **Clip It**—Shingle and gutter clips can take a little time to install, but they create unmatched straight lines. To use, hook them to lights first, then to the gutter or shingles.

- **Cords**—Use only outdoor-rated extension cords that are insulated well and include a third prong to reduce electrical risks.

- **Play It Safe**—Avoid shocks and shorts by keeping electrical connections dry.

- **Upgrades**—While that old string of lights your grandparents used and passed down to you might look nifty, think about upgrading to LED (Light Emitting Diode) lights. LED lights are long-lasting, often designed to glow for tens of thousands of hours. They're durable and made of acrylic that's hard to break. Because LED lights stay cool to the touch, they aren't as likely to start a fire. They also allow you to use fewer extension cords because you can connect several times more strings together than you can with incandescent lights.

- **Double Up**—For maximum lighting impact, hang two strings of lights in each location, staggering them so the bulbs glow close together.

LUMINARIES

There's nothing quite as pretty as candlelight flickering on freshly fallen snow. But if you've ever made luminaries out of paper bags and had them tip over and catch on fire, you'll be happy to know there is another, less pyromaniac, option.

These luminaries are simple to make and will illuminate the outdoors without any fire hazards if you use battery-operated candles.

Supplies needed include a can, a nail, a hammer, tape, and a pattern, unless you are good at winging it freehand.

STEP 1: Start with a clean, empty can. You can use any type of metal or tin can, but make sure the edges where it was opened are smooth. If you don't want to clean out a can or are worried about sharp edges, you can purchase empty quart-size paint cans at most hardware stores or online. Fill the can nearly full of water and freeze several hours until hard.

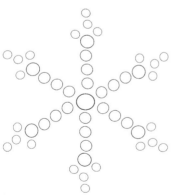

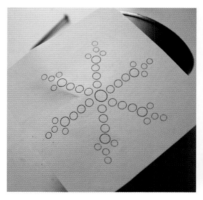

STEP 2: Choose a design for your luminary. If you print out a pattern, look for a simple dot design.

STEP 3: Remove the can from the freezer and brace it somewhere it can't roll. Tape the design to the can.

STEP 4: Using the design, punch in the holes of the pattern with a hammer and nail. The ice absorbs the blows from the hammer, keeping the can from compressing or the nail from poking through the other side on smaller cans. Remove the ice and pattern, insert a candle, and enjoy.

DO YOU WANNA BUILD A SNOWMAN

If you've ever struggled to make a snowman that didn't look like a blob someone had shoveled off the front walk, don't worry! With a few tips, you can make a snowman that'll be the envy of the neighborhood Frosty experts.

A little planning goes a long way in building an epic snowman.

❄ Choose a location that is shaded to keep your snowman intact as long as possible.

❄ The best snow for building snowmen happens right at the freezing point. If snow is too dry, spray a fine mist of water over it. You don't want it too wet, though, so go easy if you do add water.

❄ Begin the process by forming a snowball with your hands. Add more snow until it's too big to hold. At that point, start rolling it on the ground away from you. Change directions as you roll, to make the snowball as big in circumference as possible.

❄ Flatten the top of the snowman's base. Roll your next snowball, making it slightly smaller, then flatten the bottom before stacking on the base. Flatten the top of the middle section, then roll a smaller snowball for the head. Flatten the bottom of it before placing on the middle layer.

❄ If the snowballs are too heavy to lift (lift with your legs, not your back!), you can create a ramp. Just place a board on the base and roll the middle snowball up the ramp into place.

❄ Once your snowman is assembled, pack snow between the layers to help hold everything together. You can also push a stick vertically through the center of the snowman to give it stability.

❄ If you, or a family member, have creative talents, use kitchen tools like butter knives or serving spoons to sculpt details.

❄ To help slow down the melting process, mist your finished snowman with water to freeze the outer layer of snow.

❄ Decorate your snowman with old clothes or hats. You can use old plants for hair, peppermint discs for cheeks (the snow will turn pink beneath them and give the snowman a rosy hue), and rocks for eyes if you don't have any coal. You can also add solar-powered LED lights for eyes or buttons to make him glow at night. If you decide to go all Calvin and Hobbes, food coloring in a spray bottle works great for creating eye-catching interest.

❄ Don't forget to give your masterpiece a name!

TRIM THE TREE

I THINK I PROBABLY DROVE MY MOTHER BANANAS every December during my childhood years asking, "Is it time yet?"

It wasn't Christmas I was so eagerly looking forward to, but our family's annual trek to the woods to get our Christmas tree. The tradition was established long before I joined the family, but it was one we continued for years and years. Generally, two weeks before Christmas, we'd pile into our vehicles and head out on a long drive to the woods.

Often, my dad and brothers would cut a load of firewood while Mom and my sister-in-law got the fire going and made lunch. After stuffing ourselves with hot dogs, chili, and cookies, we'd buzz around on snowmobiles, searching for the perfect Christmas tree. Once we'd found trees for everyone on the list (which could include aunts and uncles, grandparents, or anyone who wanted one and couldn't join in the fun), we'd head back to the vehicles and enjoy more snacks.

I must have been about seven or so the year my oldest brother brought along an impressive selection of soda pop and made everyone snow cones. It was the best snow cone I've ever had!

Then there was my last year of college when I'd broken my foot a few days before Thanksgiving. Rather than do the sensible thing and stay home with my foot up, I pulled on multiple pairs of Dad's wool socks over my cast, wrapped my foot and leg in a garbage bag to keep the cast dry, and went along. When the doctor removed the cast, it was full of pine needles. Hmm . . . how did those get in there?

I wouldn't trade those wonderful adventures for anything, or the sweet memories I have of each excursion.

courtesy of Shana Bailey Photography

JUSTIN AND SHANA BAILEY

THERE'S JUST SOMETHING MAGICAL ABOUT THE MOMENT you plug in the Christmas tree lights and the warmth illuminates not just your home, but also your heart. Suddenly, Christmas is there in each twinkling little spark of brilliance, in decorations wrapped in memories, and in the joy of shared traditions.

For an eastern Oregon family, their annual trek into the woods with friends to cut down a Christmas tree is one tradition they look forward to all year.

"We go Christmas tree hunting with neighboring ranchers who have young children," said Shana Bailey of Pilot Rock, Oregon. "We go up into the mountains where the snow is deep and cut Christmas trees for ourselves, and also for employees, friends, and family who can't go. There's a campfire. We cook hot dogs and drink hot chocolate. Usually, we go about two weeks before Christmas."

Shana and her husband, Justin Bailey, along with their two children, live on the ranch where Shana was raised. The couple own Bailey Performance Horses. They also work with her father, Terry Anderson, who owns Anderson Land & Livestock and the 7Up Bull Program. And Shana has a photography business, too.

With so much going on in their busy everyday lives, Shana said the holidays provide the perfect time for their family to reconnect.

"I love when the kids are home and we're all together," Shana said. "We crave the weekends and the holidays when we can be together."

Shana met Justin in 2001 in Pendleton, Oregon. Justin, who grew up in Carey, Idaho, and has been training horses since his teen years, already had a degree in equine science from the College of Southern Idaho in Twin Falls. He'd moved to Pendleton to finish his business degree at Blue Mountain Community College and compete with the school's rodeo team.

At that time, Shana had returned to the family ranch after obtaining a degree in agriculture business at Oregon State University in Corvallis. One memorable day, she happened to meet Justin at the Rainbow Café, a restaurant and bar that has been in business since 1883.

The couple wed in 2003 and moved to Marsing, Idaho, where Justin worked as an assistant trainer for Dan Roeser of the Roeser Ranch. Shana worked in risk management at Agri Beef Co., in Boise, Idaho, during the week and spent the weekends cheering for Justin and Dan at horse shows.

Their son, Easton, changed their lives forever when he arrived in 2006 on Christmas Day.

"My favorite thing about Christmas is our son was born Christmas Day. Easton is just a gift from God, and his birthday makes the day so special," Shana said. "Easton loves to hunt, fish, and participate in sports," she said. "He's very passionate about sports and extremely athletic."

In 2009 the family welcomed Ali, who hopes to be a fashion stylist and superstar cowgirl. According to Shana, "Ali is wild beyond even Easton's imagination." Ali loves to ride and train horses and enjoys the day-to-day activities on the ranch.

"The kids are very different from each other," Shana said.

When Shana's father was diagnosed with cancer, she and Justin moved to the ranch in 2010 to help out.

"It all just came together at the right time," Shana said. "Being here is meant to be."

Due to Justin's rigorous training schedule, the nonstop work of a thriving ranch, and Shana's own photography business, they all look forward to the holiday season when life gears down a little.

"Holidays are really the only time we have to slow down and be together," Shana said.

courtesy of Tamera Kenyon Photography

The Bailey family eagerly anticipates breakfast Christmas morning. Cindy Gallaher, Shana's mother, comes then and makes Swedish pancakes from a recipe passed down from Shana's paternal grandmother. "I can't ever remember not having them Christmas morning."

Christmas Eve, the family gets together at the home of Shana's brother, Corey. "We celebrate Easton's birthday then. Corey's house is so warm and inviting, and it breaks things up for Easton to celebrate his birthday that day."

Shana and Justin feel it's important to teach their kids about giving, too.

"I take the kids to the school, and we get a list of things for a family in need, then purchase the gifts together," Shana said. "Christmas was getting out of control with too many toys and clothes, so we started giving to charities or a needy family. We usually buy a cord of wood to give to someone anonymously."

Shana said a special Christmas memory is the year she and Justin helped someone who'd never celebrated Christmas. "It was amazing to help them experience Christmas and celebrate the season for the first time."

The Bailey family enjoys getting outdoors during the holidays for a little fun.

"We are professional sledders!" Shana said with a laugh. "Here at the ranch, Justin will pull the kids behind horses. When it snows, it makes a lot of extra work. We try to make some fun with the snow instead of focusing on the extra work it creates."

And a big part of that fun is their annual excursion to find the perfect Christmas tree.

"Always, we have at least a twenty-five-foot Christmas tree. Our living room has really tall ceilings and I want the tree to touch the ceiling," Shana said. "Everyone is always laughing about my Christmas tree. My dad would cut trees like that when I was growing up."

She said it isn't always easy to decorate the tree, but worth the extra effort. "We decorate the top while it's down, then stand it up to do the rest because the ladder won't reach the top."

Although she doesn't have one favorite ornament, Shana said she loves the ornaments they put on the tree.

"My mother has handed down all our ornaments we made as children. Our tree is one of those that's decorated with ornaments that are handed down, ornaments we've bought for our kids that we'll give to them one day, ornaments they've picked out each year. I like that, I really like that tradition. Our kids are still young enough that Christmas is such a magical time for them, and for us, too."

CHOOSING THE RIGHT TREE

THERE ARE A WIDE VARIETY OF FRESH TREES OUT THERE, and sometimes it can be hard to decide what to choose. Do you want one with a fabulous fragrance? One that holds its needles longer? Long needles? Short needles? Skinny or full? Since we live in one of the top Christmas tree–producing states in the country, we've never had trouble finding one we love. We prefer those with a pleasant fragrance and dense foliage.

My husband will never let me forget the year I wanted a pine tree that reached the tall ceiling in our new home. The tree was too big for our stand and top heavy, too—a horrible combination if you have breakable ornaments. After it tipped over (for the umpteenth time) in the middle of the night and startled us out of a peaceful slumber, Captain Cavedweller set an anchor bolt in the wall and wired up the tree. We never had another tree tip over, but it was challenging to hide that ugly bolt the rest of the year!

Here are some tips for finding the right tree for you, particularly if you are shopping in a tree lot:

- **Fitting your family.** Each tree species is a little different, so match the tree to the needs and wants of your household. If you have little ones at home, lean toward pine or fir trees with soft needles rather than a sharp-needled spruce.

- **Freshness matters.** Bend a needle in half with your fingers. A fresh fir should snap. Fresh pines bend but should not break.

- **Test the needles.** To find a tree that will last through the holiday season, reach inside the tree, grab a branch, and gently pull your hand toward you. The needles should stay on the tree, not come off in your hand. You can also tap the end of the tree on the ground and see how many needles fall off. The fewer, the better.

- **Go green.** Some varieties of Christmas trees will go from rich green to a dull gray-green if they get dried out.

- **A fresh slice.** Once you choose your tree, take off about an inch from the bottom of the tree's trunk (tree lots will often do this at no extra charge). The fresh cut allows the tree to absorb more water and hold its needles longer. As quickly as you can after making the cut, get your tree into water.

- **Measure twice, cut once.** We've all been there. The tree that looked so perfect in the woods or at the tree lot has somehow doubled in size on the trip home and won't fit inside the house. Rather than hacking away at it, make sure you measure twice before you choose a tree.

- **Keep your cool.** Heat sources, including fireplaces and heating vents, dry out trees at a rapid rate. To keep your tree fresh and green, keep it away from heat.

- **Thirsty trees are good.** The more water a tree drinks, the longer it will stay fresh. Make sure you keep plenty of water in the stand, checking it a few times the first day or two in particular.

TREE VARIETALS

Sometimes it helps to know the types of trees available. Here's a quick guide to some of the most popular choices:

- **Noble Fir**—The Cadillac of Christmas trees. Needles on this tree vary from dark green to bluish green and turn upward. Noble firs generally have excellent needle retention and sturdier branches that extend outward, perfect for heavier ornaments.

- **Grand Fir**—The most fragrant choice in the world of Christmas trees. Needles are glossy, dark green in color, and flat along the branch. Needle retention is similar to Douglas fir trees.

- **Douglas Fir**—One of the most popular Christmas trees on the market. Short, bright green needles fill the densely branched trees. Due to uniform shape, pleasing fragrance, and lower price, it's a perennial favorite.

- **Fraser Fir**—A wonderfully scented choice for a tree. Dark blue green in color, the branches turn slightly upward. Fraser fir trees offer good form and needle retention.

- **Balsam Fir**—Needles are known to last a long time. With a dark green appearance, balsam firs generally retain their pleasing fragrance throughout the holiday season.

- **White Spruce**—While grand for hanging ornaments, the needles can emit a bad aroma when crushed. The trees are bluish green and offer excellent foliage with a good natural shape.

- **Colorado Blue Spruce**—Excellent needle retention is a hallmark of this tree. Needles are bluish gray, sharp, and can be a bit smelly when crushed. The tree has good symmetrical form.

- **White Pine**—The largest pine in the United States. This tree features soft, bluish-green, flexible needles. The trees have good needle retention, little aroma, but aren't recommended for heavy ornaments.

- **Virginia Pine**—Among the most popular tree choices in the South. Stout, woody branches respond well to trimming. Foliage is dense.

- **Scotch Pine**—One of the most common choices for Christmas trees. Typically, the needles don't fall off the tree even when dry. Bright green, the tree is known to remain fresh throughout the entire Christmas season.

- **Leyland Cypress**—The most popular Christmas tree in the Southeast. Dark green gray in color, the Leyland cypress has very little aroma. Because it is not in the pine or fir family, it does not produce sap.

TIPS FOR TRIMMING THE TREE

Year ago I volunteered with a philanthropic organization that put on a festival of trees every year to raise funds and collect donations for needy families in the community. Not only was it a fantastic charity, but the time I spent helping with the festival taught me a number of tricks and tips for adding an extra dose of "Wow" to Christmas trees.

Follow these tips to make your tree the most beautiful one you've ever had!

- **Filler**—If your tree is a little sparse (but not quite Charlie Brown status), you can create a fuller appearance by tucking artificial garlands into the bare spots. You can also use dried floral fillers like baby's breath, German statice, caspia, or broom bloom.

- **Illumination**—Lights play a key role in adding oomph to the overall look of your tree. Place one strand of one hundred mini lights or twenty-five large bulbs for every foot of height on your tree. Rather than wind strands around and around the tree, drape the strands back and forth along the branches, making sure you get inside by the trunk as well as near the branch tips. This provides illumination throughout the whole tree instead of just at the end of branches.

- **Garlands**—Whether you're using ribbon, sparkly garland, cranberries, popcorn strings, or twine, make sure you plan for approximately nine feet of length for every foot of the tree. Again, don't just toss the garland around the edges. Weave it through the branches for the most impact. Arranging it diagonally or vertically can provide a unique focal point, too. If your tree is on the skinny side, use a thinner, lighter garland. If it's a dense, heavy tree, go wide.

- **Ornaments**—Plan on about twenty ornaments per foot of tree. If you are going to run short on ornaments, supplement with inexpensive items like candy canes or pinecones. Place smaller ornaments near the top and gradually increase the size to have the larger, heavier ornaments near the bottom.

- **Tree Toppers**—A good rule of thumb is to leave eight to twelve inches between the tree topper and the ceiling. For a tree under five feet, you want a four- to six-inch topper. For trees in the five- to seven-foot range, look for a six- to ten-inch topper. If your tree is over seven feet tall, take the height times 1.5 to determine the size of your topper. For example, an eight-foot tree could have a twelve-inch topper.

- **Tree Skirts**—The height of the tree should determine the size of your tree skirt. You don't want a tiny tree swimming in yards of skirt. On the opposite end of the spectrum, you don't want a towering tree to look like it's wearing a tutu with a skirt far too small. A good rule of proportion is for every foot of tree, you need six to eight inches in diameter of tree skirt. A six-foot tree would look good with a thirty-six- to forty-eight-inch tree skirt.

Clippings Tree

If you have a live tree, you're most likely going to have some clippings and branches left after it's been trimmed and a fresh cut made on the end. Take those extra branches and pieces and turn them into a fresh mini tree. You can also make the tree with artificial branches.

This tree is a snap to make and will look amazing anywhere you place it. Use floral foam cut into a cone shape for fresh branches (and make sure to keep it moist), or use a regular foam cone for artificial greens.

SUPPLIES:

Branches

Wire cutters

Foam

Flower pot or container

Floral tape or floral putty

STEP 1: Place floral putty in the bottom of the container, or use floral tape to secure foam. (If using live branches, soak the foam in water so it's moist before you get started.)

STEP 2: Find your "top" piece and stick it in, then, working up from the bottom, begin poking branches into the foam. Use larger, heavier branches at the bottom, graduating to smaller pieces as you near the top. If you are using artificial greens, think about blending a few different kinds to give the tree a more natural look. Continue until foam is covered.

CINNAMON ORNAMENTS

When Captain Cavedweller and I were newly married and trying to make every dollar stretch as far as possible, I made a batch of cinnamon ornaments for our tree. Mercy! They filled our little home with the most wonderful, decadent scent and were a fun accent for our tree. I still have a few of those ornaments, even all these years later. A hint of cinnamon lingers on them, as well as many special memories. This recipe is simple, takes no time to make, and is perfect for youngsters to help with.

Makes approximately 2 dozen ornaments

1 cup all-purpose flour

½ cup salt

½ cup ground cinnamon

¾ cup warm water

STEP 1: Combine all ingredients.

STEP 2: Knead the dough with clean, dry hands. If the dough is too sticky to knead, dust your hands with flour. As you begin kneading the dough, be prepared for the aromatic wafts of cinnamon to nearly make you swoon.

STEP 3: Roll or pat dough out flat until it's about ¼ inch thick.

STEP 4: If you have youngsters in the house, this is a great time to get them involved. They can cut out shapes to their heart's content.

STEP 5: When you're finished cutting out the dough, pierce the top of each shape using a straw or skewer. This will create a hole to thread a ribbon through later.

STEP 6: Place the ornaments on a rack or parchment-lined tray to dry. (If you put them on a tray, plan to turn them multiple times to ensure both sides are drying.) Allow to dry for about 24 hours.

STEP 7: Thread ribbon or string through holes and hang on the tree.

Note: *You can paint the ornaments if you like (acrylics work best), but I like to leave mine au naturel.*

ORNAMENT STORAGE

If you're like me, when it's time to pack up the Christmas decorations and put them away, there's a bit of sadness that the holidays are over. And there might even be a wave of relief that the house will soon be back to normal (whatever that is!). As you pack the decorations, make sure they are clean, any broken parts are mended, and everything is organized. You'll be so glad you made that effort when you open up those boxes next holiday season.

Follow these easy tips to get your tree trimmings organized for next year!

- **Lights**—Use the empty cardboard rolls from gift wrapping to keep lights untangled. Simply tuck the plug inside one end and secure it with a piece of tape. Wrap the strand around the tube, then tape the other end of the light string inside the opposite end of the tube. I've packed lights this way for years and I never have any tangles.

- **Fragile**—Small ornaments that could easily break do well in empty egg cartons.

- **Plastic Cups**—Those bright red cups are useful for more than holding party beverages. Wrap ornaments in tissue paper then slip one inside each cup and stack them in a storage tub for a quick and inexpensive way to protect ornaments.

- **Bubble Wrap**—I used to spend what seemed like half of forever carefully packing ornaments back into the little foam molds they came in. Then I'd have white foam pieces all over everywhere that no amount of vacuuming could fully contain. Do yourself a favor and buy a roll of bubble wrap. It does as good a job of protecting your cherished treasures, doesn't leave behind a mess, and takes no time at all to unwrap when you're ready to decorate.

- **Bows**—Keep bows from being smashed by stuffing each loop full of crumpled tissue paper.

- **Ornament Containers**—If you want to keep your treasured ornaments in something better than egg cartons and plastic cups, you can purchase plastic tubs or storage boxes with dividers specially made for ornaments. I was fortunate enough to receive one as a gift a few years ago and I love it.

SONGS OF THE SEASON

CAROLING CAN BE SUCH A SWEET, JOYOUS WAY to celebrate the season with others. One of my fond childhood memories was going caroling with my best friend's family and members of her church. It was so, so cold, but we had a wonderful time. People plied us with treats and hot chocolate. Afterward, we returned to the church where we enjoyed sugar cookies and fellowship.

Whether caroling is something you look forward to every year, or something you think you'd like to try for the first time, you'll enjoy reading about one family who has made it a special tradition.

And don't miss the tips on organizing your own caroling event!

courtesy of Renee Moss

HANK AND RENEE MOSS

MANY FAMILIES HAVE SPECIAL TRADITIONS during the Christmas season that they look forward to each year. The Moss family of Prineville, Oregon, has a unique Christmas tradition that started as a way to make the holiday more memorable for their three young children.

"One of the greatest traditions that we started with our children was Christmas caroling on Christmas Eve," said Renee Moss. "When Hank and I were first married, we did everything we could to go home to southern Utah for Christmas. There finally came a time that we just couldn't afford to make the trip. With three small children, it was just too hard to pack everything up to take with us, so we decided to spend Christmas at home. We still wanted to make it special, so Hank and I decided to visit some of our friends and give them a song. The kids were one (Sadee Jo), three (Wyatt), and five (Jozee)."

courtesy of Renee Moss

The couple did encounter a slight problem, though. The only song Jozee knew by heart was "She Wore a Yellow Ribbon." Not exactly standard caroling music, but that didn't deter Hank and Renee.

"I baked a bunch of sweet bread loafs to disperse with each visit and we bundled up and started knocking on doors," Renee said. "When the doors opened, we all broke into song at the top of our voices and gave them our finest rendition of 'She Wore a Yellow Ribbon.' Tears of laughter met us, but the kids thought everyone loved it and just sang even louder! The next year we started a few weeks earlier and learned an actual Christmas carol, but ended each visit again with 'She Wore a Yellow Ribbon.' Through the years, we have added many traditional Christmas carols."

All three Moss children have been involved in music, but the boys now play with many groups throughout central Oregon, and with their own band, Moss Brothers Music. Their talents add a special element to the family's musical traditions.

courtesy of Renee Moss

"With the boys being very accomplished musicians, we added an accordion and then a mandolin to our caroling, but always end with a rousing rendition of 'She Wore a Yellow Ribbon,'" Renee said. "The best part of this tradition is seeing the smiles as we break into the Yellow Ribbon song."

Renee said friends who have been caroled to more than once through the years always anxiously wait to see if the family will sing the song. When they do, many join in.

"One of my fondest memories was of a Christmas we spent in Wisconsin," Renee said. "We were very homesick for our central Oregon friends. A few days before Christmas, a package arrived containing a video of many of our dear friends at a church Christmas social. In it, they sent small messages of Christmas greetings, and all joined in to sing the Yellow Ribbon song to us!"

To this day the Moss family continues its caroling tradition.

"This is still how we spend Christmas Eve. Our daughter Sadee Jo now is the master baker and bakes up yummy treats that we can share with our listeners. There is an open invitation to whoever would like to join us. We are always ready for hot soup and candlelight when we get home."

It only seems appropriate that Hank and Renee, and their children, have such strong Christmas traditions. After all, the couple spent their first date decorating his Christmas tree.

"Hank and I met in southern Utah. He was a local bull rider and I was the current county rodeo queen," Renee said. "I was working in a convenience store that he frequented a lot."

Renee invited Hank to a concert she and some friends were planning to attend.

"I asked him if he would like to come along. He said yes, but about a week before the concert he asked me to come over to his place and help him decorate his Christmas tree," she explained. "Yes, the first official date was decorating Hank's Christmas tree."

The couple wed a year later on November 25, 1989. Their first Christmas tree as husband and wife was decorated with flowers from their wedding cake.

"When we were able to get a larger tree, I made lace ornaments to accompany the flowers," Renee said. "The tree was simple but beautiful and reminded us of our special day."

Renee explains that many of their holiday traditions are a combination of customs she grew up with as well as those she and Hank thought would be fun.

"The traditions that we kept going were traditions I remembered growing up. They were pretty simple and payed homage to coming from a very poor background," Renee said. "My grandparents, Joe and Vernie Wren, left Iowa during the Dust Bowl and moved to California as newlyweds. They didn't have a lot, but they always had family and put the emphasis on family ties."

One tradition her grandparents started that Hank and Renee continue is a candlelight dinner of oyster stew on Christmas Eve.

"This was something we did faithfully with my family growing up, with a break now and then of potato soup. We have continued this tradition every year. With our children, I added a chicken club brunch ring along with the soup, but the idea is of the simple soup that was so treasured and was a feast for my grandparents. The candlelight also gave the sense of peaceful reflection and how thankful we need to be not only for the food we had to eat but the ability to have electricity and a warm home," Renee said. "Many blessings that can be easily taken for granted."

Christmas morning finds the Moss family going through their Christmas stockings followed by opening presents.

"We take the time to have each person open their presents while everyone else watches. This ends up taking the whole of the morning, and we are famished by the time we are finished," Renee said.

The traditional Christmas breakfast they enjoy is one passed down by Renee's parents. At a time when money was tight and there wasn't a whole lot to go around, hunting was necessary and provided fresh meat for the winter.

"My dad grew up in a small town in southern Utah and enjoyed the abundance of game meat that his family lived on," Renee said. "The most common way to cook it was to thinly slice the meat, dip it in flour, and then fry it in bacon grease. Most families in those days were lucky if they owned a milk cow and were able to enjoy the abundance of fresh milk and cream. A simple gravy was made by warming up the skimmings off the cream from the milk, then seasoning it with bacon grease and salt and pepper. The gravy was made in the pan with drippings from frying the venison slices. The gravy was then served over toasted bread (sourdough is our favorite) and the fried meat simultaneously. This delectable entree was what was passed down as our traditional Christmas breakfast. By the time we finish with this simple meal, we are so stuffed we are all ready for naps."

Books are another important part of the family's traditions. When their children were young, Renee and Hank looked forward to reading to them.

"Every year I would buy a new book to read on Christmas Eve. If it was a chapter book, I'd start reading it in the weeks

courtesy of Renee Moss

before Christmas," Renee said. "This was so much fun, and some of my best memories as a mom come from reading to my children. I loved that time with them."

Hank and Renee also shared their love of the meaning of the season through another book that was special to them.

"We were introduced to a beautiful Christmas story a few years before our kids were born titled *The Forgotten Carols* by Michael McLean. This story touched us so deeply that we try to share it with as many folks as we can," Renee said. "Every few years, we plan an evening before Christmas and invite friends over for the reading. Hank reads the story and we play the songs on the accompanying CD. The story lasts about three hours and sets the mood and the priorities that we need to have with keeping the focus on what Christmas really is all about."

CAROLING, CAROLING

WHETHER YOU'VE CAROLED EVERY HOLIDAY SEASON FOR YEARS, or want to try your hand at something new that sounds like a wagon load of fun, a little planning goes a long way when it comes to Christmas caroling.

Dress for the weather. Comfortable shoes are a must. If you're going to be out in chilly winter air, dress warmly, bring blankets for those who don't, and have Santa hats or reindeer antlers on hand for those who really want to get into the spirit of the event.

Illumination. For those houses you visit that are blacker than Scrooge's heart on Christmas Eve, carry flashlights. Stock up on glow sticks, too. They're great to wrap around the wrists and ankles of young children, making them easy to keep track of, and visible in traffic, too.

Music is a must. Not everyone can be expected to remember every single verse to all the carols you plan to sing. Bring sheet music to share. Cover the basics like "Jingle Bells, and "Silent Night," but also add in some nontraditional tunes like "Leroy the Redneck Reindeer" or "I'm Gettin' Nuttin' for Christmas."

Bring drinks. Keep those singing pipes hydrated so you can hit the high notes. Bring a thermos, or four, of apple cider or hot chocolate, along with bottles of water.

Plot a course. Caroling is a wonderful way to connect with neighbors and friends, but don't forget about the elderly or shut-ins who would enjoy a little holiday cheer.

Set the time. No one will appreciate being interrupted in the midst of dinner, so start caroling after dinner, but early enough that younger children won't already be in bed.

Loving from your oven. Bake cookies, quick breads, or other treats to share not only with fellow carolers, but also with those you visit as you carol.

WRAPPED IN LOVE

EACH YEAR I CAN FEEL THE ARRIVAL of the holiday season. It doesn't come in a loud burst of excitement. Nor is it found in the chaotic cacophony of shoppers seeking bargains while fighting for parking spaces and growing increasingly Grinch-like as they stand in lines that stretch half of forever.

It isn't in a lone object or specific moment that signals the season of joy has descended, but in a million little things all tied together.

To me, Christmas floats in gently, softly, with a feeling of nostalgia and warmth, edged in fond memories and filled with possibilities.

It's like having a loved one drape a soft blanket around you, surrounding you in its embrace.

Quite simply, the season arrives wrapped in love.

That love is evident in the story of a sweet couple just beginning their happily-ever-after.

You can find it in presents beautifully wrapped with care.

And you'll experience it through gifts given to those who open their home and say "come celebrate the season with us."

NICK AND MEGAN LADUKE

THERE'S NOTHING LIKE A BUDDING ROMANCE to wrap the holiday season in love, even for a rodeo cowboy.

Professional Rodeo Cowboys Association saddle bronc rider Nick LaDuke grew up in Livermore, California, but had moved to Houston, Texas, to pursue his professional goals. In 2012 he came home for the holidays and met the woman he would marry.

The night before Christmas Eve, a mutual friend introduced him to Megan Baughman.

"I was downtown with my best friend at our local dive bar, and Nick walked in with two guys that we were both friends with," Megan LaDuke said. "We started chatting and I was instantly attracted to him, but not too sure about him at first, living in Texas and all."

But Nick eventually returned to Livermore, and the couple wed in 2016, a few days after Thanksgiving. That first meeting, so close to Christmas, makes the holidays an even more special time of year for the couple.

courtesy of Nick LaDuke

"I love Christmas time in general, so meeting around that time is a nice feeling to add to it," Megan said.

Nick, who sometimes doesn't arrive home from the rodeo circuit until just before Christmas, said connecting with family over the holidays is one of his favorite parts of the season. "To be able to relax and catch up with family without time constraints is great."

Although they both grew up in town, Nick and Megan embraced the western lifestyle from young ages.

Megan's grandparents had a ranchette in Livermore, making it possible for her to compete in barrel racing, cutting, and breakaway roping in junior and high school rodeo. Her mother was a barrel racer and former rodeo queen, and passed that love of rodeo on to her daughter.

One of Megan's favorite Christmas gifts during her teen years came from her grandfather.

"My grandpa bought me a brand-new roping saddle when I was in high school. I really needed it to rodeo," she said.

For Nick, his rodeo career began when he was just six years old and rode a calf at a junior rodeo. His mom, Sue McKinnon, was a fan of rodeo and took him to the Cow Palace near San Francisco when he was "just tiny," and his love of rodeo took root.

"I always loved horses," he said. After issues with grand mal seizures, he wasn't allowed to compete for several years, but by the time he was a teen, he was back to competing. He was able to make a choice of which high school he wanted to attend. A talented golfer, he could have pursued golf, but chose instead to attend a school that offered FFA and rodeo programs.

courtesy of Sue McKinnon

By the time he was fifteen, he knew he wanted to compete professionally in rodeo. "I rode bulls and horses, got several injuries, and decided on saddle bronc riding."

Nick spent time with relatives in Kansas learning more about horses while his dream of competing professionally evolved. He attended the University of Las Vegas in Nevada and graduated with a bachelor's degree in sociology, determined to have a backup plan to his career goals.

Megan pursued a career in an entirely different industry, and has a hairstyle and makeup artistry business.

Nick and Megan recently purchased eight and a half acres near Knightsen, California, less than thirty miles from where they grew up. They both fell in love with the area after exploring it.

"We are putting a house on it, and an arena and barn. We named it Agape Ranch," Megan said. "I am looking forward to our future kids being able to grow up in the country, and for Nick to have a space to run his horse business and help kids get started in rodeo."

Nick, who had to learn so much about rodeo and riding by trail, error, and injury, is dedicated to mentoring youth and helping them.

"I love how passionate he is," Megan said. "He brings out the best in me, and makes me a better person. He has the ability to do that in people and animals. He is very focused and driven in achieving whatever it is he wants. He has had a lot of physical injuries/setbacks and always pushes through them."

courtesy of Nick LaDuke

Those injuries and setbacks are part of what inspires Nick to mentor others.

"Coming from town, from a broken home, without many resources, I got a lot of injuries from jumping in without proper training and background. I want to be the guy who helps others grow and be successful and use rodeo for what it's worth. Rodeo isn't just a country sport. It's so much more that can be taken in whether you're from the city or country," Nick said. "If you do good for others, it will come back around into your own life. I want to help young people learn."

Nick already does training and riding for others, working with problem horses. He plans to have an equestrian training facility along with a rodeo training facility that focuses on animals and athletes on their property.

In 2015 Nick sustained a major injury that left him unable to compete while he healed. The Justin Cowboy Crisis Fund stepped in and provided assistance until he was back on his feet.

"It's scary getting hurt and not knowing how you are going to pay your bills. JCCF really helped us out in a hard time, and gave us peace of mind," Megan said.

Nick, who is good at public speaking, joined forces with JCCF, helping with fund-raisers, radio promotions, and camps. Giving back to others is something Nick learned from his mother, Sue, who gave him a love for the holidays.

"Mom was a single parent and didn't have a lot of extra money. Right after Thanksgiving, she'd start making cinnamon rolls and give them to anyone who'd helped us, or been a part of our lives," Nick said.

In addition to cinnamon rolls every year, Nick said Christmas traditions from his childhood included going to church services on Christmas Eve, then coming home and opening a gift of new pajamas.

A picture of the perfect Christmas for Megan is "having our own family one day, and celebrating opening presents and eating good food at our own home."

"I'm looking forward to our future together, to creating new traditions," Nick said. "Megan is the best gift I've ever received. She slows me down and helps me see what Christmas is all about, what it all should mean to me."

GRANNY'S CINNAMON ROLLS

Sue McKinnon, Nick LaDuke's mother, shared her memory of Christmases past—and her recipe (see page 154):

"Every Christmas friends would bring Nick and me cookies and in turn I would make cookies to give to our friends. Exchanging cookies is such a fun and loving tradition for the holidays. However, I realized around January 1, I would throw dried, tired cookies away. Nick had his fill of cookies. I thought, hmmm . . . if I am throwing away these thoughtful gifts, I bet other people throw away our cookies, too.

"Thanksgiving 1986, I started giving great thought to baking cookies for the holidays. I was a single mom with a very active two-year-old little boy (Nick LaDuke). With money very tight for me, I wanted to have something for Nick and me to give our friends, but I didn't want something that everyone else was giving. The epiphany hit me! My grandmother-in-law (also known as Granny) used to make cinnamon rolls for us, and they became my most favorite homemade treat!

"Beginning the first week in December 1986, I started baking Granny's Cinnamon Rolls recipe. The first year I gave away approximately twenty trays of cinnamon rolls as Christmas gifts. So it began . . . the new tradition. They became so popular I would have friends asking in October if I was going to bake the rolls. One Christmas, I gave away fifty trays of rolls as Christmas gifts.

"Over the years, our older friends have passed away, but a new generation is now enjoying the sweet gift. It was fun hearing how my rolls became part of our friends' Christmas traditions. If I gave them early before Christmas, they would freeze them for their Christmas morning tradition.

"Jim McKinnon joined Nick and me in 1988. He enjoyed our tradition, too, and enjoyed participating in the baking experience. A new tradition for our household began. . . . On Christmas Eve as we were heading to Concord to join Jim's family for Christmas Eve, we would make special stops to deliver rolls to our older friends. Their smiles and warm hugs will be in our memories forever."

THE PERFECT PACKAGE

THE EXCITEMENT OF FINDING JUST THE RIGHT GIFT for someone special never grows old. No matter what is inside the box, though, when a present is beautifully wrapped, the recipient will be smiling long before he or she uncovers the gift.

I've always enjoyed wrapping gifts. In fact, when my mother discovered how much fun I had doing it, she turned over all wrapping duties to me. A few years, I even wrapped my own gifts after Mom taped the boxes shut and made me promise not to peek. When my husband and I first wed, his idea of wrapping a gift was a brown paper bag sealed with duct tape. He has since discovered in-store gift wrapping!

Admittedly, I am a wrapping paper snob. If it isn't good-quality paper, I won't use it, but the reality is that a little ingenuity is all that's needed to add flair to your gifts. One of my favorite methods of accenting a package is to top it with an ornament I know the recipient will like. You can add natural elements like greenery, berries, pinecones, or even feathers. Tie a bandana into a bow. Use twine as a ribbon. Spurs, bits, and strips of leather look great on packages, too. Just remember, no matter how you decorate the gift, make sure it is wrapped in love.

STAR BOW

Years ago, I happened upon the directions for a unique package topper. It's easy to make, rather like cutting out a snowflake, and never fails to bring a little pizzazz to a special gift. All you need is a ruler or measuring tape, wrapping paper, tape or glue, and a sharp pair of scissors.

STEP 1: Wrap your gift. Measure across the width of the box. Cut a square of paper approximately an inch or two smaller.

STEP 2: Fold your square of paper in half vertically, then horizontally until you have a smaller square.

STEP 3: Fold your square into a triangle by folding in half diagonally.

STEP 4: Trim off the edge of the square so the top of your triangle is rounded.

STEP 5: Cut up each fold line, almost to the tip, being careful not to cut through the tip.

STEP 6: Place on a flat surface and unfold until you have eight sections.

STEP 7: Fold the sides toward each other, overlapping, until it forms a cone. Tape or glue to hold in place.

STEP 8: Continue with all eight sections. Place glue or tape in the center.

STEP 9: Position on top of gift box and press in the center. Continue making layers, each a few inches smaller than the last.

SUPER CYLINDER

Once in a while, a gift comes in such an odd little shape, nothing seems to fit it. Make this cute cylinder for bearing gifts from a chip can, paper, and double-sided tape. Tuck round or oblong gifts inside or use it for edible delights like cookies, candy, pretzel sticks, beef jerky, or popcorn.

STEP 1: Cut a piece of wrapping paper the width of the chip can, making it long enough to overlap about an inch on the length.

STEP 2: Place double-sided tape along the top and bottom edges of the can. Place a small piece to anchor a center point on the vertical edge, then carefully roll the paper around the tube, pressing it into the tape. Place a strip of tape along the outside vertical edge of the paper and press down.

STEP 3: Add a bow, ribbon, or ornament to finish your creative design.

GIFT TAGS

To add another personal touch to gifts, think about creating your own gift tags. Blank craft tags with jute ties can be found at most craft stores and are inexpensive to purchase.

Decorate them with rubber stamps, washi tape, fabric designs, conchos, or ribbon.

Look for holiday or western cardstock and make tags by tracing shapes with cookie cutters and cutting them out (this is a perfect activity to keep little hands busy!).

Playing cards also make a fun gift tag. Just punch a hole in the top, add string or ribbon, and attach to your gifts.

You'll also find dozens of downloadable patterns online for gift tags. Print tags on plain card stock, cut out, add a string or ribbon, and you're ready to accent those packages!

HOSTESS GIFTS

IT'S ALWAYS A LOVELY GESTURE and good idea to take a gift to your host or hostess. Not only will it be appreciated, but it may come as a welcome surprise to your hosts to be thanked for their graciousness with a memorable token of gratitude.

You could choose from any number of gifts to express your thanks for their kindness, but here are some ideas.

SMALL AND SWEET [SMELLING]

If you're traveling and don't have much room in your suitcase for a gift, think about giving your hostess a small decorative box with essential oils or aromatherapy bottles inside. To add a little extra something special to your gift, nestle the bottles between the folds of a gorgeous winter scarf or silk wild rag.

If you've never heard that term, a "wild rag" is a western scarf worn by both men and women. They come in a variety of sizes, colors, and fabrics, although silk and polyester are among the most popular choices. Wild rags date back to the 1800s

when cowboys used them for warmth in cold temperatures and for protection from the sun, wind, and dirt. They also used them to strain drinking water, make a sling or bandage, wrap a coffeepot handle, drape over the eyes of a spooked horse, start a race, blow a nose, or temporarily tie something together. Wild rags aren't just for fashion purposes!

THE BREAKFAST BASKET

A wonderful gift for a hostess is a breakfast basket so she won't have to think about fixing a meal the following morning. Choose a nice, large basket like this one, lined with fabric that she can reuse or repurpose. Fill it with a selection of seasonal whole fruits, juice, milk, holiday tea (one of my favorites is Stash's Christmas Morning tea), coffee, or even hot chocolate mix. Add muffins or quick bread, like banana bread, which my husband can't leave alone when it is warm and fresh right out of the oven. You might want to include a container of spreadable cream cheese or whipped butter to go with the bread. And I'd include a package of bacon and breakfast links from Hill Meat Company (hillmeat.com), who do delicious things with smoked pork.

TIED UP WITH STRINGS

Aprons can be a creative and well-received gift for the hostess (or host) who likes to cook or has an apron collection. Choose from traditional holiday patterns like holly and berries, poinsettias, holiday plaids, and snowflakes, or go a little crazy with a bolder print. If you're handy with needle and thread, make your own. Patterns for aprons are generally easy to follow, and you can find an exciting assortment of fabrics like bandana prints, southwestern prints, bucking broncs, adorable little cowboys, and even fabric that looks like tooled leather.

COASTERS

We've found over the years of attempting to save our tabletops from water rings that you can never have too many coasters. Think about giving your hostess a set of coasters as a special gift.

Agate coasters are ruggedly beautiful. If you aren't equipped to slice your own agates, then look for natural pieces that have not been colored (the dye can leach into wood) and are backed with cork to absorb moisture.

Another fun option for coasters is to make them out of leather, or purchase them premade, too.

You can use horseshoes and cork to create coasters. Just cut a piece of cork to fit, then glue it to the horseshoe.

A great place to find cork already cut to the perfect coaster size and backed is in the garden department of stores. Look in the planter section among the planter trays and saucers. You'll find cork discs in a variety of sizes, but the smallest one is perfect for coasters. To personalize it, add a brand or initial.

FRESH HERBS FOR THE KITCHEN

Fresh herbs are a gift that can be appreciated long after Christmas if they are potted.

Rosemary makes a beautiful mini tree. Other herbs you could include are sage, mint, and dill. Tarragon, thyme, and basil make fantastic options, too. Purchase herbs to plant at home, then repot in small containers to give away. One of our local grocery stores even carries herbs with roots in the produce section to make it easy to get started on an herb garden at home.

SCENTED SUGARS

If you're searching for a unique hostess gift and your hostess knows her way around the kitchen, think about making scented sugars.

Most everyone has mixed cinnamon and sugar together (what better topping for toast!), but take that idea a step further with a variety of ingredients.

Scented sugar adds a subtle undertone to beverages, desserts, and baked goods. Layer granulated sugar with aromatic edibles like lavender, mint, orange or lemon zest, rose petals, or vanilla beans.

To begin your project, sterilize jars and dry completely. Small four-ounce jars are a perfect size. Wash the aromatics and let dry, then mix with sugar, seal in jars, and allow a few days for the scents to infuse the sugar. A good ratio is about one-half to one teaspoon of aromatics to each quarter cup of sugar. The scent of the zested orange in that little jar was enough to fill my entire kitchen with a decadent, knee-weakening scent when I removed the lid.

A GIFT OF WRAP

For the hostess who may have last-minute gifts to wrap, put together a basket filled with everything she needs for wrapping gifts. Include a pair of pretty scissors she'll enjoy all year. Search for uncommon wrapping paper to make the gift even more special, like this Fredrick Remington printed gift wrap. Include an assortment of gift bags and tags, as well as rolls of ribbon and a few little trims like jingle bells—and don't forget a roll of tape.

THE PAMPERED HOSTESS

No hostess would turn down a basket full of items meant for pampering her. Choose quality candles, look for lotions and bath products in holiday scents, and don't forget to include a loofah or bath sponge. Tuck in an eye gel mask that can be left in the refrigerator for a cool and refreshing treat for a harried hostess. Add candy and a gift card for coffee.

HOME FOR THE HOLIDAYS

THE HOLIDAYS, FOR MANY, can be about loading up and heading out to visit family or friends, or it might be about staying home and opening your door to loved ones. Regardless of where you hang your hat on Christmas Eve, one thing is for certain—home is where you find your heart.

Discover how one couple from Oregon celebrates going home for the holidays and learn a few tips for making the most of time spent with guests in your home.

JUSTIN AND TONA ANDRADE

THERE'S NOTHING QUITE LIKE COMING HOME for the holidays, regardless of the location.

For Justin and Tona Andrade, home is where their loved ones are gathered. Some years find them in New Mexico with Tona's family to celebrate Christmas. A recent move to a small community in eastern Oregon puts them closer to Justin's family.

"We take turns going from Justin's family to mine," Tona said. "The Christmases when we go to New Mexico are amazing. Being away from my family most of the year is hard. I come from a very close family."

Tona anticipates time spent reconnecting. "I stay up with my sisters, reminiscing, laughing, and sharing memories. It's so nice to all be together," she said. "With everyone spread out, it's rare that we are all together. When we are together, we celebrate family in a big way. It's all about putting everything else aside and spending time together. There's a feeling of warmth, love, and comfort when everything stops for a while and everyone is together."

Justin echoes her feelings about spending the holidays with loved ones.

"I love being with family members we don't get to see all the time," Justin said. "It's great to see our kids and how they look forward to the Christmas holidays."

Tona grew up in New Mexico and has participated in rodeo since the tender age of five. With a dad who competed in team roping, calf roping, and steer wrestling and a mom who raced barrels, rodeo was in Tona's blood. Her parents trained horses, including five horses her dad trained that made it to the Wrangler National Finals Rodeo in three different events.

She competed in barrel racing in high school rodeo, and then in college in West Texas where she also played basketball. Due to her drive and talent, she earned national titles and was among the competitors three years at the WNFR. The horse she rode, Moe, was one trained by her mother.

One spring, she found herself in California for a series of rodeos and needed a place to keep her horses. At the time, Justin was also competing in rodeos while living in Livermore, California.

"I remember when she came out for the spring run that year. She was beautiful and she was a champ," Justin said. "I had a buddy tell her she could keep her horses at my place so I could get to know her."

courtesy of Tona Andrade

It didn't take long for them both to realize they'd met someone special. After dating for four years, they married in 2006.

Justin competed professionally in rodeo and in Professional Bull Riders events for around eleven years, riding all three roughstock events. He attended college on a rodeo scholarship with a goal of winning Rookie of the Year in bull riding. An injury to his knee cut his year short, but he returned the next season, ready to ride.

During the years of his rodeo career, Justin broke several bones, from a leg to an eye socket. In 2002 he qualified to compete at the WNFR, but on the opening night, a bull tossed him on his head. With two herniated discs, he was unable to continue competing.

"Justin was out of competition for a long time," Tona said. "The Justin Cowboy Crisis Fund contacted us and offered to help. Most rodeo cowboys have families, and there isn't a lot out there to help them if they are injured. The fact that the JCCF comes in and helps athletes who've dedicated their lives to this sport . . . I don't have words for how great it is."

Twice, the JCCF has offered a hand up to Justin and Tona. The first time was after his neck injury in 2002. When the couple found out they were expecting their son Chase, Justin retired from bull riding. A few years later, he was helping with a bull riding clinic for youth and ended up reinjuring his neck in the same place while trying to keep one of the students safe.

The trauma of the injury left him paralyzed for a brief time. Doctors put in a plate, and Justin recovered.

"For the JCCF to step in when you're down like that is just amazing. All the stuff that goes through your mind when doctors say you won't walk again . . . to have them step in and help is such a big deal," Justin said. "They've helped us out a lot over the years, and I want to give back."

Which is what he does through his involvement with the Professional Rodeo Cowboys Association youth rodeo.

"It's my way of giving back. When I was young and getting into rodeo, there were guys that I really looked up to, but they wouldn't take the time to spend with kids," Justin said. "I like helping kids learn, helping them get better. I stress getting an education, and surrounding themselves with winners and good people."

Tona said one of the things she most admires about her husband is the way he "commits to what he does. He's very passionate about things that are important to him. And I admire the way he is a father to his kids."

Justin admires Tona's positivity. "She is a champion when competing," he said. "There's no negativity when she was competing, and she's the same woman today. She's very positive and she's just a good person."

Now that he's officially retired and Tona dabbles in competing, they are focusing on a new chapter in their lives on eighty acres they purchased in 2018 near the small town of Nyssa, Oregon.

"Family and business opportunities drew us here," Tona said.

A typical day for the Andrade family includes chores, checking the cattle, getting the kids off to school, horse training, and school activities. Tona said if time permits she loves to get in a ride with daughter Maddy in the afternoon.

Christmas gatherings often find them riding with family, too.

courtesy of Tona Andrade

"We go out and ride in the snow, take the kids tubing," Tona said. "My family has an indoor arena, and we also ride there. With eight grandkids in my family, we like to play in the snow, get outside, and do something fun."

For Justin and Tona, Christmas isn't about what's beneath the tree, but who is gathered around it with them.

"Everyone is happy around Christmas," Justin said. "Christmas is about being with our family. Watching our kids Christmas morning is just priceless."

Home is Where You Leave Your Heart

WELCOME HOME

WHEN CAPTAIN CAVEDWELLER AND I FIRST MOVED AWAY from our families, we couldn't wait to go home for the holidays and see everyone. There's just something magical about the moment you walk through that door, knowing people are waiting to see you, lavish you with hugs, and all talk at once, eager to catch up on news and life and just being together.

To enjoy a visit to its fullest, here are a few helpful tips:

Minimalize travel stress as much as possible. If you're upset when you arrive at your destination, it can be hard to get back to a happy place during the visit.

Master the art of conversation. Small talk with people you rarely see can be awkward. A few relatives probably drive you nuts. And you'd rather hide in a corner with your phone than have to listen to Uncle Frank tell *that* story one more time. But stow the technology, remember why you're with family, and turn those awkward conversations into opportunities to learn more about someone you might not know well.

Keep expectations realistic. Between nostalgia over the splendor of the holidays when you were a child, the magic of the season, and the hope that things will be perfect, we can sometimes create unrealistic expectations of time spent with family. Approach the visit with a healthy dose of realism mixed with optimism.

Focus on the joy of family. They know you. They love you. Find activities you can do together that everyone enjoys, or break into smaller groups to keep everyone busy, involved, and having fun.

SPECIAL GUESTS

There are special guests who come to stay during the holidays that we just can't wait to welcome to our home. Make sure their visit is as pleasant as possible with advance planning. They'll appreciate the extra effort made to make them feel pampered and cherished.

Start by finding out information from your guests such as:

- How many nights will they be staying?

- Do they have any allergies—food, pet, etc.? This is very important to know!

- What are their favorite foods, beverages, magazines, books?

- What activities interest them?

- Give your guest room a test run by spending time in the room. You may even want to spend a night sleeping there to make sure the shades or drapes are adequate, the heating vent is open, and the pillows are comfortable. You'll get a much different perspective by spending the night in the room than you would just walking in to make sure everything looks clean and inviting.

- Once your guests arrive, encourage them to feel at home by showing them where the necessities can be found. Stock some of their preferred snacks and beverages.

- In the guest room, provide a few magazines or a book by their favorite author. You may also want to have a tray with a note of welcome, bottled water, and mints or chocolates. Fresh flowers are also a welcome touch.

- Show them where to find extra pillows and blankets.

- The guest bath should be stocked with plenty of fluffy towels. It is a nice touch to put out a tray or basket with sample-sized toothpaste, cotton swabs, new toothbrushes, shampoo, and conditioner for any of those items your guest may have forgotten.

- Provide adequate lighting at night in hallways with nightlights.

- Keep a list of area attractions, restaurants, and other local items of interest available for your guests. If they are staying more than a few days, they might like a dinner on their own or some time to explore.

- Make sure you are available to your guests without smothering them. With a little planning, you can relax and enjoy your time together!

CHALLENGING COMPANY

No matter if you're traveling to stay with family for the holidays or welcoming out-of-town guests to your home, everyone can have a holly jolly holiday with thoughtful preparation.

One of the biggest challenges for anyone is dealing with difficult guests. We love them dearly, but Uncle George likes nothing better than to strike up a good argument, Aunt Nelda is critical of everyone, and little Tiffi really does think she's a princess.

Nip problems in the bud with these simple tips:

- Encourage everyone to go outside and get a breath of fresh air before dinner. If you can get them engaged in a game of touch football, or building a snowman, or going for a horseback ride, even better. The combination of fresh air and wearing them out tends to make for mellow guests.

- A guest who is bored may soon grow critical, nitpicky, and unpleasant. Maybe Uncle George can sharpen the knives, or put Aunt Nelda to work folding napkins or chopping veggies for a salad. Even younger ones can be given tasks like taking coats or making place cards.

- Plan ahead where you'd like everyone to sit at the table. Place hearing-impaired guests next to loud talkers. Place the politically opinionated in the midst of children. Strategic seating makes for drama-free dining.

- If the guests arrive a day, or four, before Christmas, have tasks to keep idle hands (and minds) busy. They can help wrap gifts, decorate, make ornaments, run to the grocery store, and so on.

HOT CHOCOLATE STATION

There's just something warm and cozy about holding a mug of steaming hot chocolate in your hands. Set up a hot chocolate station to greet those who've been playing outdoors or anyone who enjoys a cup of holiday joy.

Start by setting up an area dedicated to your hot chocolate station. Make sure you have plenty of mugs available and within easy reach.

You can make a batch of chocolate and serve in carafes or beverage servers to keep warm, or simply have hot water and let your guests mix their own chocolate. If you let them mix their own, offer a variety of chocolate flavors to choose from, like dark chocolate peppermint or caramel.

Have a tray full of goodies they can add into their drinks, such as marshmallows, whipped cream, peppermint and cinnamon sticks, mini chocolate chips, and sprinkles. You can also have flavorful extracts or, for the adults, liqueurs available to add in. Let your imagination run wild!

Make sure you have plenty of spoons and napkins handy.

For an added element of fun, spear marshmallows with peppermint sticks, dip in melted chocolate, and top with sprinkles to stir into warm mugs of liquid deliciousness.

SPILLS

If you have company at your house, stains and spills are inevitable. To handle some of the most common holiday stains, follow these tips:

Candle Wax—Let the wax cool or place the item in the freezer for a few minutes. Gently pry off hardened wax with a knife or spoon. Place the fabric between layers of paper towels and press with a warm, dry iron, rotating the towels as they absorb the wax. Rub in liquid detergent. Wash in warm or hot water with fabric-safe bleach.

Pumpkin—Scrape off excess and flush with cold water. Rub in liquid laundry detergent or pretreatment spray. Wait five minutes, then wash in the hottest water that's safe.

Cranberry Sauce—Rinse with cold water. Soak for fifteen minutes in a mixture of one tablespoon white vinegar, one teaspoon liquid detergent, and four cups cool water. Launder as usual.

Tree Sap—Soak in rubbing alcohol to soften, then peel off what you can. Work in more alcohol to dissolve any remaining stain. Rinse. Rub in laundry pretreater and wash in the warmest water safe for the fabric.

Wine—The specialty cleaner Wine Away is great to have on hand to treat stains from red or white wine spills. Otherwise, cover the stain with salt. The salt should absorb a red wine stain and turn pink. Then soak the stained fabric in cold water with an enzyme detergent overnight and launder as normal.

Grease—The best tool I've found for removing grease from fabric is Dawn dish soap. Rub it right onto the stain then rinse with cool water. Repeat as necessary until the stain is gone. Launder as normal.

...es take your choice.
...heartily rejoice

With best Christmas Wishes

POST CARD
FOR ADDRESS

...how your
...Clems snow...
...? I've been flow...
...working up until...
...now And it...
...to quit I'll wri...
...when I get time...
...Sunday...
...the tide

Dear Hester, Most...
Am sorry we could...
get something real...
This space may be used for communication.
...hope to have some...
...thing later on...
...a good...

Chris
Gre

I'm glad to send this car...
With greetings and go...
And hope when Christmas...
You'll be as glad as an...

PRESERVING MEMORIES

FOR MANY, THE HOLIDAY SEASON is a time full of nostalgia as we recall sweet memories from the past. We might spend more time remembering those who are no longer with us during Christmas. And we reflect on how grateful we are for the loved ones around us.

It's important to capture these moments while we can. Preserving memories is something we all can do. Everyone can snap a photo or two, but think about taking your efforts to another level.

Our memories are actually connected to all our senses: sight, taste, smell, hearing, and touch. Think about ways you can capture memories that evoke each of these senses. Maybe it's baking something from a recipe passed down for generations. It can be the smell of a particular holiday scent. I know a whiff of bayberry makes me think of my grandma like nothing else can.

A wonderful way to save cherished moments from the past is through a quilt or pillow made from a beloved shirt or dress, even a pair of jeans! It's not just seeing the fabric incorporated into something new and wonderful, there's also the feel of the material.

Take the time to gather oral histories from those who are growing older. Encourage them to jot down their memoirs and break out the photo albums.

While you're recalling past memories with loved ones, you're sure to make new ones to treasure.

courtesy of Carla Harrison

JOHN AND CARLA HARRISON

KNOWN AS THE "CLOWN FAMILY" in the rodeo world, John and Carla Harrison don't clown around when it comes to the holidays. In fact, this couple and their children have found unique ways to preserve meaningful holiday traditions and integrate them into their celebrations.

"I find it fun to come home after being in Las Vegas for the first two weeks of December, and in one day turn the house into a Christmas wonderland," said Carla Harrison. "John usually gets out his grandparents' old turntable; we listen to vinyl Christmas records and I put on a boiling pot of cranberries, oranges, and cinnamon to make the house smell like Christmas."

John and Carla, as well as their children—Addy, Caz, Billie (who passed away in 2014), and Charlee—are regulars on the rodeo trail, but each December finds them in Las Vegas for the Wrangler National Finals Rodeo.

John knew at a young age he wanted to be a rodeo entertainer and barrelman.

"I was always interested in trick riding and I got a lesson from J. W. Stoker and then went to Karen Vold's school," John said. "That, paired with my father teaching me how to trick rope, gave me the basis for a specialty act. I got my PRCA card in 1999 and started my rodeo career. John Walter of Mid States Rodeo was my first rodeo run."

John's first captive audience was for a 4-H talent show in his teen years. The success of that inspired him to continue. "I'm the barrelman and entertainer at rodeos. During the bull riding, I hop in my Coors Barrel and pro-

courtesy of Carla Harrison

vide an island of safety for the bull riders and bull fighters. I like to be there to help a man out, and the front row seat to watch the bull riding is awesome! My kids all like it when their dad gets hit in the barrel! The rest of the rodeo, I devote to entertaining the crowd. I try to use unscripted banter with the announcer and the crowd to keep things moving. I have several acts that I haul with me, and we use those throughout the rodeo."

With a large repertoire of skills, John has done everything from roman riding to trick roping. The industry has recognized John's unique talents, too. He was selected by his peers to be the 2013, 2015, 2016, and 2018 Wrangler National Finals Rodeo Barrelman. He received the title of Coors Man in the Can in 2014, 2016, and 2017. Additionally, he's been named Comedy Act of the Year by the Professional Rodeo Cowboys Association.

John grew up on the family ranch his late grandfather, world champion bull rider Freckles Brown, purchased in the 1950s.

"Growing up in rodeo, and always having rodeo people around, made me aware of all aspects of rodeo, and it was the specialty act/entertaining side that piqued my interest," he said.

It was while he was working for Steve Gander's World's Toughest Rodeo tour based out of Iowa that he met a California girl who would change his life.

At the time, Carla worked as an intern doing publicity for the World's Toughest Rodeo and caught John's eye. The internship ended, but their relationship was just beginning.

Carla grew up in Salinas, California, where her parents ran cattle and were involved in farming. Her dad was also known to do a little roping and ranch rodeoing.

After John invited her to attend the PRCA awards banquet with him where he was nominated for Specialty Act of the Year in 2004, Carla realized she was in love with him.

"I admire John's fairness in all situations and how he puts others before himself," Carla said. The couple wed in 2006.

When asked what road led her to where she is today, Carla laughs. "I'm still trying to figure that out! It had to

courtesy of Carla Harrison

be divine intervention, because who else thinks about marrying a clown?"

As often as they can, Carla and the children go with John on the road. School has kept them closer to home, and Carla has her own business to work around, too, as an auctioneer.

One of the benefit auctions Carla looks forward to each year is the Pro Rodeo League of Women Style Show & Luncheon held at the South Point in Las Vegas. The event raises funds for the Justin Cowboy Crisis Fund.

According to John, "Carla is hard-working in every endeavor, a great mom and wife."

When they aren't on the road, life at the Harrison home is still hectic.

"We run cattle, juggle an auction schedule, own a liquor store and a bunch of rental houses," Carla said. "There's not much down time. Did we mention we have three kids, two with sports and 4-H?"

However, Christmas holds a special place in the hearts of the Harrison family for many reasons.

"I love decorating," Carla said. "It is one of the only holidays we are all home, so we like to go all out. We also always cut a live tree off the ranch—it's kind of a Charlie Brown tree, but it's our tree."

When it comes to the decorations for the tree, John recalls memorable ornaments from his childhood.

"Our church would sell Christmas ornaments, and my mom would get one every year with our name and the year on it. We still put those on our tree," he said. They also treasure ornaments they have in memory of their daughter Billie.

Carla finds ways to include other meaningful items into their celebrations, as well.

"I like to incorporate platters and decorations from John's grandparents and my parents, all of whom have passed."

Even the fireplace mantles in their home hold sweet memories. "John's grandparents planted their first Christmas tree in front of the house, and it grew there until just last year. We now are enjoying it as our mantles and not cursing all the needles we were constantly sweeping."

Carla and John have three words to sum up the holiday season: love, family, and faith.

"It's the time of year everybody is home and able to enjoy a holiday together and celebrate the true meaning of Christmas with family," John said.

CAPTURE MEMORIES

ONE OF THE BEST WAYS YOU CAN PRESERVE MEMORIES is through photographs. While most people today have cameras constantly at their fingertips with their cell phones, it's nice to have a professional portrait taken from time to time. However, getting ready for a family photo shoot can be a little stressful. Jamie Brown, a professional photographer from eastern Oregon, shares tips for a smooth photo session.

When to plan. It is best to book outdoor family sessions from May through October. Outdoor sessions are typically held a few hours prior to sunset. Book a month or two in advance to ensure the date of your choice, especially later in the year when the sun sets earlier and weekend appointments are favored.

Setting the mood. Your photographs are designed to be displayed in your home, whether artfully showcased on a wall or placed proudly on a shelf or table. When having portraits taken, think of where you'd like to put these photos and the overall sense of style in that room. What mood does it portray?

Location. Is there a spot around town that your family frequently visits, a place you drive by every day and are inspired by its beauty? If so, *that's* where you should have your photo shoot! The right location can make a big impact on the overall look and feel of your photo.

What to wear. Consider color tones and how these represent the feeling and style you want to convey. Try to pair colors and coordinate outfits of family members for a cohesive look. Layer textures, colors, and patterns and accent them with jewelry or accessories like watches, scarves, or hats. All these layers can give a polished appeal to the overall look of the photos. For kids, let their personalities shine through their wardrobe choices. Allowing them freedom to express their own personal styles within the colors you've chosen for the entire family is fun and keeps everyone looking consistent without appearing too matched.

Extra outfits and accessories. If session time allows, bring wardrobe changes. Young children are notorious for making messes on their clothes.

Backup shoes. A lot of locations are off the beaten path in grassy fields or pastures with manure, so a sturdy pair of walking shoes or boots to wear to the shoot is a good idea. Change into the fancy shoes once you get there.

Makeup or hairbrush/accessories. Ladies: Touch-ups for lip gloss, a bit of blush, and some powder are a must! Bobby pins or hair ties are also a good thing to have on hand. Fellas:

A comb or lotion for dry hands is about all you'll need aside from items that coordinate with your outfit (hat, belt, tie, etc.).

Wet wipes. Come in handy during any type of session, especially with young ones.

Any prop or special item. Discuss beforehand with the photographer. If including a family pet, bring a crate or carrier for them when not in the photo. Bring water and treats as well as something that makes noise that is unexpected (a bag of potato chips or marbles in a can) to perk ears up and grab their gaze at the right moment.

Other things to consider:

Manicure or pedicure. Don't forget that sometimes your hands will be posed by your face; a coat of nail polish (even clear) is something to consider before your shoot. At the very least, remove the chipped remains from your last coat of paint.

Haircuts or hair color. Roots with color grown out two inches down from your crown, bangs that hang down past your eyes, or fuzzy hair all down your boy's neck may need some attention prior to your photo shoot.

Be confident. The best thing you can bring to your photo shoot is confidence. When you are open to the process and authentic, you're guaranteed to make some beautiful memories!

PHOTO MEMORIES

Photos taken of friends and family over the span of generations are priceless treasures. As our loved ones age, it can be hard for them to remember past people, places, and events. Yet, sitting down with a photo album will sometimes open up a deep treasure chest of memories. Cherish and capture those times by preserving not just the pictures but also the words your loved ones share. Ask questions about anything

and everything related to a photo, then write down your discoveries. Encourage your family members to record their memories, whether in print or video. Share favorite old songs to jog memories—hum, sing, or whistle. Dancing is optional, but foot-tapping is required.

PHOTO GIFTS

Gifts that are personalized with photos are a wonderful way to not only preserve memories, but share them, too. There is just something about a photo gift, created with a meaningful photo, that makes such a unique and beloved present. Last year I took a photo, circa 1980-something, that was captured at the family farm Christmas Day and had it turned into a puzzle for my dad. He loves to do puzzles, and it was great to give him a gift of a fun day spent with our extended family.

The options for creating photo gifts are vast and varied. You can personalize everything from dish towels and potholders to pillows, blankets, mugs, ornaments, and clocks. And don't forget about the joy of receiving a scrapbook! The only real limit on a photo gift is your imagination.

PHOTO ORNAMENT

Save a cut from the bottom of your Christmas tree to make a memorable ornament, or purchase a wood slice from the craft store.

SUPPLIES:

Slice of wood

Modge Podge

Scissors

Photo

Drill

Ribbon

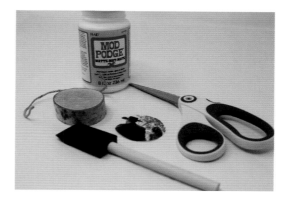

STEP 1: Cut a photo to fit just inside the ring of the wood slice.

STEP 2: Brush a layer of Modge Podge over the wood, then place photo on top. Allow to dry for 15 to 20 minutes.

STEP 3: Brush with another coat of Modge Podge. Allow to dry. Apply additional coats as needed.

STEP 4: Drill or punch a hole through the wood slice near the top.

STEP 5: Thread ribbon through hole. Your ornament is ready to hang on the tree!

PAPER CHAIN

MOST EVERYONE HAS MADE A PAPER CHAIN to count down the days until Christmas. I remember Mom letting us take out wrapping paper Thanksgiving evening, and we'd count how many pieces we'd need then cut the strips and glue them together. It was such fun to remove the links, knowing each one that we tore off brought us a day closer to Christmas.

This idea for a paper chain is the opposite. Instead of tearing away links, you add to them each year. Have family members write one memorable or special thing about the holiday season and date it, then link the chains together. The next year, add to it, and the next. Young and old alike will enjoy adding to this unique paper chain, and it will bring to mind special moments of past holidays as you read through the notes on each link. All you need to make this is wrapping paper, double-sided tape or glue, scissors, and pens to write the messages.

CHRISTMAS CARDS

EACH YEAR AFTER THE HOLIDAY SEASON ENDS, I save all the Christmas cards we've received, tucking them into a resealable bag and storing it with the decorations as I pack them away. It's fun to look through the greetings when we get out the decorations the following holiday season, but that's not the reason I hang onto the cards. Because I refuse to throw them out, I have the last Christmas cards our grandmothers sent as well as aunts who are no longer with us. When I get out those special cards each year and see the notes written inside the cards in their handwriting, I'm ever so glad I kept them. Think about saving your cards, at least until next holiday season, because you never know when it might be the last one you receive from someone you dearly love.

MADE FROM THE HEART

ALTHOUGH I CAN'T KNIT TO SAVE MY LIFE, my efforts at crocheting typically result in a mile-long string, and my quilting attempts appear like a drunken chicken has grabbed the needle and headed to town, I do enjoy making gifts for others.

There's just something about creating a special present for a loved one that fills my heart with anticipation and joy. Will they like it? Will it be something they treasure? Will they know how much they mean to me through that particular gift?

One thing I've discovered is that when I create something unique for someone, or even have something personalized for someone, it's that extra effort that makes the gift precious to the recipient.

Because I'm well aware of my crafty limitations, I'm glad there are people in this world—like one amazing couple from eastern Oregon—who can make nearly anything!

If you can wield a glue gun (or a bottle of craft glue), there are easy-to-make wreaths, ornaments, and gift ideas you can create. And even if you are all thumbs when it comes to crafts, having a gift personalized has never been so simple.

Just remember to share gifts from the heart this holiday season and you won't go wrong.

DEREK AND JESSICA MILLER

ONCE IN A WHILE, AN UNANTICIPATED GIFT comes our way and changes the world around us. For one eastern Oregon couple, the unexpected happened May 5, 2013, when they met at Hot Lake Springs, a resort and foundry near La Grande, Oregon. Derek Miller was already employed there, but a young woman named Jessica arrived that day to interview for a job in the bronze foundry.

Jessica nailed the job interview and soon began working there, although it wasn't until December of that year when she and Derek went out on their first date.

"The biggest thing that drew me to him was our shared interests and ability to work together as a team," Jessica said. "Not to mention that he was handsome and had an amazing smile!"

Derek said he felt a connection to her in a variety of ways. "We both have a love of horses and the western/ranching lifestyle, the outdoors, photography, animals, and art. We had similar goals, and it was easy to see that we made a great team."

They wed in August 2016 and "have yet to spend a single night apart," Jessica said.

Both Jessica and Derek have roots in the country that derive from their youth. While Jessica said her family moved often when she was growing up in Oregon's Willamette Valley, her grandmother owned a small acreage near Molalla where she has fond memories of visiting.

"That is where I grew my roots for the love of the farming and ranching way of life," Jessica said.

For Derek, his country roots grew from his family's homestead in eastern Oregon, near Elgin. His grandfather passed away when he was sixteen, and his family moved to the timber and cattle ranch to help his grandmother.

"We lived thirteen miles from town, and it really cemented my love for country and ranch living."

Derek and Jessica moved to Baker City, Oregon, in March 2014, and bought the place where they currently reside.

Between the two of them, there isn't much they can't make or create. They own several small businesses together, including Ranch Studio Artworks. Jessica started RSA after graduating from college.

"When I met Derek, he challenged my abilities and brought even more to the table as well as encouraged me to start an online presence."

Derek said before he got involved with RSA, Jessica "did really cool western art and decor. When I came on board, the products evolved with a mixture of both of our styles and influences. We still do some of the same things, but have added many new items and do a lot of custom work."

Jessica said one of the first things she discovered when she began showcasing her original artwork was her lack of marketing skills. She started creating practical and affordable functional items, like horseshoe hooks, that the average person could afford and appreciate.

"Together, we have realized there is no project that we cannot do, so now we offer anything from custom cowhide furniture and custom leather products such as belts, cuffs, holsters, and chinks to picture frames, horseshoe letters, cake toppers, clocks, lamps—you name it!"

courtesy of Jessica Miller

Derek added that their offerings encompass home decor, art, leather goods, and photography.

One of the areas where Jessica's talents particularly shine is painting and sculpting.

"Painting has always been a passion of mine; however, it can be time consuming, and the older I get, the less I am finding myself able to sit still for too long. Building with my hands has always been very rewarding, and with sculpting I am able to see the results I want much faster."

The couple has worked on fascinating projects of all sizes, although Jessica says some large projects have been challenging.

"One in particular was a life-sized impression/relief of a bugling elk out of barbed wire. When starting a project like this, it is very intimidating, taking something so thin and destructive and turning it into something amazing. Then there is always the challenge of how to display it."

They agree the elk project was one of the most "challenging and exciting projects that we built together," Jessica said.

The holiday season is their busiest time of year, although they've steadily built their year-round online sales through outlets like Etsy.

courtesy of Jessica Miller

"Holidays can get pretty busy with online orders, especially with creating our own custom gifts for our friends and family," Jessica said. "Luckily, in the wintertime, it's cold outside and snow usually covers the ground, so it creates a perfect environment to bring out the creativity and time to spend inside working on projects."

The holiday season is a special time for the Millers.

For Derek, it's all about family. He said Christmas is a time for "the ones we get to see, the ones we don't, and the ones that are no longer with us."

"When I think of Christmas I automatically think of the colors, smells, family, and the time to think of others," Jessica said. "Snow was a bonus if we ever got it growing up. Now that we live in Baker, the snow is just the icing to the cake! Having four true seasons really helps with getting into the holiday spirit."

They agree an ideal Christmas celebration would include unlimited time with family.

"The perfect Christmas to me would be our families all in one place for a week at least with lots of snow," Jessica said.

HEARTFELT GIFTS

D O YOU HIT PANIC MODE WHEN IT COMES to finding the perfect gift for your friends and family? Is your go-to gift of choice gift cards?

While I'm all for getting and giving gift cards, sometimes it's nice to give a more personal gift, one that shows you put some thought, care, and effort into it.

Explore ideas for making simple wreaths, unique decor, or one-of-a-kind ornaments.

Even if you don't have a single crafty or creative bone in your body, there are oodles of ways you can still give a personalized gift, from a cutting board to a watch made from Grandma's old silverware.

Give a gift made from the heart, even if it wasn't your hands that created it.

Welcome Home Wreath

There is nothing quite like opening the door and stepping into a home that is redolent with the delightful aromas of Christmas. I love it when holiday scents fill our home. It warms my heart and evokes a bit of nostalgia for treasured celebrations of the past.

This simple wreath (which can also be made as a garland) is a wonderful gift to give someone, and they'll long be grateful for the lovely fragrance it brings to their home. Don't forget to make one for you, too!

SUPPLIES:

5 oranges or apples

Parchment paper

Cookie sheet

Tapestry needle with large eye

44-inch length jute string

300 dried bay leaves

Cinnamon sticks

STEP 1: Slice apples or oranges into thin slices, about ⅛ inch thick.

STEP 2: Place parchment on a large cookie sheet, then arrange fruit slices on parchment. Place in a 200°F oven for about 2 hours. Remove from oven and allow to cool.

STEP 3: Thread needle with jute and knot one end. Gently push needle through a bay leaf and slide to the end of the string. Keep adding leaves until you have about 2 inches of space filled.

STEP 4: Add a cinnamon stick (you may need to use a nail to poke a hole through the stick).

STEP 5: Add three fruit slices.

STEP 6: Repeat bay leaves, cinnamon stick, and fruit slices pattern.

STEP 7: When you reach about 36 inches on the string, tie a knot. If you want a garland, leave both ends free. For a wreath, tie knotted ends together and add a ribbon for hanging.

OTHER IDEAS FOR WREATHS

ROPE WREATH

A rope wreath is one of the simplest wreaths (and gifts) you can make. Just take an old rope no one is using (because if you take a favorite rope right out of the hands of a working cowboy, be prepared for a battle), wire it together with a piece of florist wire, then add a bow and some festive accents like jingle bells and greenery.

If you want, you could add a bandana, burlap, or non-holiday-patterned bow with a fun little cut-metal ornament or two so the wreath could be used year-round.

Sheet Music Wreath

My awesome friend Becky made this gorgeous sheet music wreath for me from pages taken out of an old hymnal. You can use any type of sheet music, and books of music found at estate or yard sales are perfect for this project. To make the wreath, all you need is approximately fifty sheets of music. Fold each one into a cone and glue it. Cut a circle of cardboard (think pizza pan circumference for a wreath this size), then glue the cones to the cardboard, starting with the bottom layer and working your way around the circle, then repeating with the top layer. In the center add whatever decoration you like best. Glue a piece of jute or string on the back for a hanger and you're ready to give a beautiful gift!

ROPE TREE

I saw a rope tree on Pinterest (one of my most favorite online places to waste time I shouldn't), and knew I had to make it. It took less than an hour from start to finish and was one of the easiest craft projects I've ever made. For extra fun, add a string of miniature lights or a tiny ribbon garland. A cut-metal snowflake topped this tree.

SUPPLIES:

Block of wood (about 3 inches square)

12- to 14-inch wooden skewer

Roll of jute string (about ¼ inch thick)

Ruler

Scissors

STEP 1: Drill or punch a hole in the center of the wood. Place a dab of glue in the hole, then set the skewer in the hole.

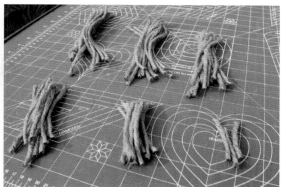

STEP 2: Cut jute into the following measurements:
12 lengths of each: 8 inches, 7 inches, 6 inches
10 lengths of each: 4 inches, 3 inches
3 lengths: 2 inches

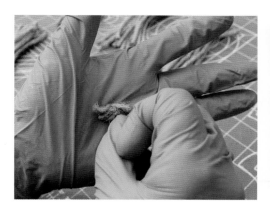

STEP 3: Fray both ends of each piece of jute. You can do this by painstakingly unraveling it, or just rub the ends against the palm of your hand. In no time at all, your hand will be sore, so you might want to wear a pair of gloves.

STEP 4: Begin layering jute on the skewer by sliding the skewer between twists of the jute in the center of each piece. Place the longest pieces at the bottom, then work your way up by size to the shortest pieces on top. Finish the tree with a topper of your choice and decorations.

Boot Christmas Stocking

Anyone would be excited to receive a stocking made just for them, especially if it was full of goodies. If you have mad sewing skills and aren't afraid to use them, you can make this stocking out of any type of fabric. Cut up an old pair of jeans and place the pocket on the front, or use plaid, camo, or a wild Christmas print to create a fun design.

If you don't even own a needle, whip out your glue and a piece of felt. Felt is sturdy enough to hang nicely, won't fray when cut, and can be glued together. Embellish with sparkles, sequins, jingle bells, or whatever accents you like.

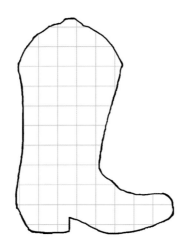

PINECONE ORNAMENT

Pinecones are versatile, making everything from centerpieces to swags a snap to create. This sweet little ornament has a snowflake shape and is simple to create. All you need are pinecones, a piece of jute, and my favorite craft tool—a trusty hot glue gun!

STEP 1: Choose six pinecones that will fit together well. Add a dab of glue to the end of one, then attach it to the next pinecone.

STEP 2: Continue gluing the pinecones together. I glued three and then the other three, then connected the two halves.

STEP 3: When all six pinecones are glued together, add a loop to hang the ornament by gluing a piece of jute or ribbon to the back side of the pinecone ornament. You can cover your glue tracks with a small pinecone glued over the top.

STEP 4: To finish your design, add an interesting embellishment to the front, like a ribbon and holly berries.

GIFTS FOR HER

If you're searching for a unique gift for a special female, you'll find some ideas here. One of my favorites is to take an old piece of silverware that has meaning, or a china plate, and have them made into jewelry. The china can be turned into earrings, necklaces, bracelets, and brooches. The silverware becomes bracelets, watches, and rings.

Handmade Soap—Whether you make your own or purchase bars, choose a scent your recipient will enjoy.

Thimble Necklace—If you have a vintage thimble from a family member who is no longer using it, think about turning it into a necklace. It will be a treasure a loved one can wear and enjoy.

Decorative Pillows—Accent and throw pillows are easy to make and can be as simple as covering a pillow form with bandanas and tying the corners together. If you're good at embroidery or sewing, create something unique for the recipient. Or shop for a pillow you'll know she'll love.

Bookmarks—Whether they are made of leather, paper, metal, or beads, an avid reader will love a special bookmark that reflects her style.

GIFTS FOR HIM

Sometimes (okay, if we're going for complete transparency about how things roll in my world, then it's necessary to say most of the time), shopping for guys can be challenging.

As in stress-inducing, anxiety-generating challenging to come up with a special gift for my husband. You'd think after all these years it would be easy, but instead it gets harder. He's got way more stuff now than he had when we were young and broke newlyweds! I still want his gifts to be personal. And so many manufacturers now offer that option with their products—add a sweet nickname or a date that's special to you both. My husband's favorite water jug even comes in a personalized option. Other ideas I've seen that have a personal touch:

- Pocket knife with exotic details like stag horn or a pinecone resin handle and engraved
- Shadowbox with toys, trophies, things of importance or from childhood
- Cut-metal art (these are especially awesome with your ranch brand or logo)
- Painted saw blades with a scene he'll love
- Custom-made belt
- Seat covers
- Wallet
- Military keepsake boxes
- Personalized ammo crate

[AND MORE] PERSONALIZED GIFTS FOR THEM

If you're looking for a gift you can give a couple, think about something a little off the beaten path, like a personalized cutting board, an ornament engraved with their names, or wine corks made from trophies. (Remove the top from the trophy, drill a hole in a wine bottle cork, add a bit of glue, insert the trophy topper, and you have an amazing, memorable gift.) Anything personalized with their name or brand that they can put on display (like a cut-metal welcome sign or a doormat) is a great option!

SHARE THE JOY

CHRISTMAS CAN BE A CHALLENGING TIME for many, especially those who have fallen on hard times and those who feel alone.

There is a variety of opportunities available to lend a helping hand during the holiday season.

A Colorado couple shares the many ways they step up and help others while teaching their daughter about the joys of giving.

The most rewarding gifts don't come from a store, but from the time and attention we share with others. It might be something as simple as shoveling the sidewalk for a neighbor, or offering to run an errand for an elderly shut-in.

Share the joy in your heart through lending a hand, volunteering, and helping out someone in need. It's a beautiful gift you'll give yourself as well as the recipient.

courtesy of Kacee Willbanks Colletti

CASEY COLLETTI AND KACEE WILLBANKS COLLETTI

THE HOLIDAYS ARE A TIME MANY PEOPLE OPEN THEIR HEARTS and wallets to those in need. But one Colorado couple believes in stepping in and stepping up year-round. Casey Colletti and Kacee Willbanks Colletti of Pueblo, Colorado, volunteer their time, skills, and effort in helping their community and beyond its borders whenever they can.

"Giving is something very important to me," Kacee said. She has helped youngsters with their horsemanship and given riding lessons.

Casey, too, has offered assistance through free bareback riding clinics online. In a live video format, he interacts with kids who want to learn more about riding bucking horses, setting up equipment, and riding techniques through Bareback Riding Online Clinic.

"With simple acts of kindness and unselfishness we will restore our faith in humanity," Kacee said. "Volunteering in my community is important to me."

Kacee puts her belief into action in a variety of ways.

courtesy of Kacee Willbanks Colletti

"To benefit the Pueblo Downtown Association, I volunteered my time to compete in the Dancing with the Pueblo Starz fund-raiser and won People's Choice for best dance. I have also volunteered my social media skills to my church and the Pueblo Country Club. Most recently, I started a fund-raiser to pay off the school lunch debt at a local elementary school. However, my most crucial volunteer experience was becoming a CASA [Court Appointed Special Advocate] volunteer. If I can perform an act of kindness that can help one person, I am happy. I would not be who I am without the volunteer work I have done."

Casey is quick to note he admires Kacee's willingness to help others as well as "her heart when she loves something and her mind when she wants to accomplish something. She is so giving and gives to strangers randomly. She's one that will send chocolate-covered strawberries to someone out of the blue or start a fund-raiser for school lunch debt at the local elementary school, and she still believes in sending handwritten thank-you notes. When people meet her, they tell her their life story within minutes. After I ride, I'll go up to the bleachers to find her and she'll always have made a new friend. We can leave the grocery store and she'll know a short version of our cashier's life before we leave."

That open-hearted outlook carries into the holidays for the Colletti family, too.

One of Kacee's favorite things about Christmas is "the feeling of 'giving' and selflessness you can feel around the world."

"We are a couple that never stops moving and striving," Casey added. "We want to accomplish everything we can and squeeze every bit out of life we can."

And often that includes being a help to others.

Casey and Kacee spent their childhoods in the same town, only a few miles apart, but didn't personally know each other.

Casey grew up with a farm background, mostly around hay and cattle. He attended amateur rodeos growing up, although he didn't come from a professional rodeo background.

Both of them attended Pueblo County High School. It was during his high school years when Casey began riding bucking horses. He qualified once for the National High School Finals.

"I went to Garden City Community College in Kansas on a rodeo scholarship and also college rodeoed for Tarleton State University in Stephenville, Texas. I won my college region while attending Garden City and qualified for the College National Finals Rodeo," Casey said. "I started at sixteen and was not an overnight success."

But he kept at it.

Kacee, however, grew up with deep roots in both ranching and rodeo.

"I come from a professional rodeo background, and my grandfather raised horses and cattle, produced rodeos, traded livestock, and provided horses for a bareback riding school with Bruce Ford as the instructor," Kacee said.

"I think Kacee has literally rodeoed almost since she could walk," Casey explained. "She always teases about how she had to pay taxes at eight years old from her winnings. She junior rodeoed and qualified three years for the National High School Finals and went to Vernon College in Vernon, Texas, on a full-ride rodeo scholarship."

Kacee was working as a social media manager in March 2014 when Casey, someone who was nearly a stranger to her at that time, reached out to her.

"Around midnight one evening, he messaged me on Facebook asking if I 'ran people's social media and stuff.' I, of course, waited until 'business' hours at eight the next morning to simply respond, 'Yes.' He then asked me if I was expensive. I couldn't pass up the opportunity for a good joke to such an awkward question, so I replied, 'Do you always ask women that question?' He was so embarrassed and quickly backpedaled to explain himself and assure me that, no, that was actually a first. Needless to say, we never discussed my social media prices and we've talked every day since."

courtesy of Kacee Willbanks Colletti

The couple married November 5, 2016, and has welcomed a baby girl, Kingslee, into their family.

Casey said the road that led him to a rodeo career "shouldn't have happened. By that I mean, compared to others competing at this level, I didn't have the kind of help or training that most did. I didn't grow up around world champions or NFR cowboys. By not learning properly from the get-go, I had a lot of trial and error."

Through his pure determination to keep entering, Casey kept an eye on competitors who'd already been to the NFR, and continued learning and trying to improve. He has now qualified three times to compete at the Wrangler NFR.

In August 2014, at the top of his game, Casey sustained a major injury at a rodeo that left him sidelined.

"I bruised my spinal cord and had loss of signal [partial paralysis] to my free arm," he said. He was told he'd never ride again and should count himself fortunate to be able to walk.

For a man who made his living through rodeo, it was devastating. That's when the Justin Cowboy Crisis Fund stepped in. The JCCF is a nonprofit organization that offers help to rodeo athletes when they are injured and unable to compete for an extended period of time.

"The JCCF was a greater assistance than I can even put into words," Casey said.

Kacee agrees. "They helped him to the point where there was time for his body to heal, rather than pushing himself to do things he was not supposed to do."

Eventually, Casey was cleared to ride again and headed back out on the rodeo road.

When they are home, they make the most of their time together. Casey said they are eager to start their own holiday traditions, especially for Kingslee. "Kacee came up with this crazy idea to buy a huge blow-up Christmas lawn ornament every year for Kingslee, so when she is eighteen, we'll have the whole yard full of Christmas blow-ups. Last year, I bought a Christmas Mickey and Minnie."

In addition to light-hearted holiday fun, the couple also reflects on matters of the heart.

Kacee said Christmas is a time to think of those who are no longer with them and appreciate those around them. "I'm grateful for my husband and my daughter, but I have strong empathy for those without family or food, or children without gifts or love."

However, the Colletti family wants to put the focus of their holiday celebration not on the gifts, but on giving from the heart.

Kacee said it's important to "give of yourself to help make others' Christmas more enjoyable. And remembering what Christmas is all about. I don't make Christmas here about gifts. Kingslee receives gifts, but I want her to learn the greatest gift of all is to give, not to receive."

READ A BOOK, HELP A COWBOY!

Back in 2013, I was knee-deep in writing the first sweet romance in my Rodeo Romance series. The hero of the story was a saddle bronc rider who sustained a debilitating injury at a rodeo. Since I'd never seen that particular type of injury in person at a rodeo, I wasn't sure how much medical care a cowboy would receive on the spot versus when he would be taken to the hospital.

Many times, I've heard, "if you're gonna rodeo, you're gonna get hurt," but I wanted to get a clear picture of what happened after a rodeo athlete was injured to that extent.

In an attempt to get my facts straight for the story, I reached out to the Justin Sportsmedicine Team®. In 1980, Dr. J. Pat Evans and Don Andrews developed the idea of a mobile sports medicine system that could provide medical support services to rodeo athletes at arenas. With the help of the Justin Boot Company, their concept turned into reality with mobile centers that link a network of selected emergency physicians, orthopedists, trauma specialists, athletic trainers, physical therapists, and massage therapists as well as hospitals and clinics around the country to provide the medical care needed for competing rodeo athletes.

The mobile medical centers annually attend more than 125 Professional Rodeo Cowboys Association rodeos, provide more than a million dollars in free medical care, treat thousands of professional rodeo athletes, and travel more than eighty-five thousand miles.

When I spoke with a representative from the Justin Sportsmedicine Team® about the information I needed for my book, they answered my multitude of questions with friendly interest and professionalism. In fact, I was so awed by the helpful kindness offered that I wanted to do a little something in return.

That's when I first learned about the Justin Cowboy Crisis Fund.

The JCCF began in 1990 when the Justin Boot Company formed a partnership with the PRCA and the Women's Professional Rodeo Association. Mindful of how traumatic injuries can be to rodeo athletes without the additional burden of financial worries, the JCCF provides a hand up when one is needed.

When rodeo athletes sustain catastrophic injuries that leave them unable to compete for an extended period of time, the JCCF is there to provide help to athletes and their families.

They've awarded more than eight million dollars in need-based financial assistance to more than a thousand injured rodeo athletes.

One thing that makes the JCCF stand out among today's numerous charitable organizations is the fact 100 percent of all contributions received are disbursed to eligible athletes. This is made possible by the joint efforts of the Justin Boot Company and the PRCA as they underwrite the administrative expenses associated with the JCCF, leaving the contributions to serve the intended purpose of assisting injured rodeo athletes.

Because of how impressed I was with both the idea of the JCCF and the work of the Justin Sportsmedicine Team®, I decided to donate a percentage of my book sales during the month of December in 2013 to the JCCF.

What began as a one-time donation has turned into an annual campaign called "Read a Book, Help a Cowboy" that provides an opportunity for me to give back to a wonderful organization. I love the country way of life, rodeos included, and this is a way for me to say "thank you" to those who inspire me through their everyday work and lives.

I hope you'll take a look at the JCCF. It's an amazing organization that really does make a difference when rodeo athletes are injured. Read the stories of Nick LaDuke, Casey Colletti, Justin Andrade, and others for examples of how JCCF has given rodeo cowboys a hand up.

VOLUNTEER

THE HOLIDAY SEASON CAN BE JAM-PACKED with one event after another. Despite what is most likely a hectic schedule, think about carving out a little time to volunteer. It's such a rewarding experience and one of the best gifts you can give because you'll reap the benefits of it, too.

Uncertain where to begin? Here are some thoughts on ways to volunteer:

Serve a Meal—The cold months are particularly hard on those who are struggling to keep food in their bellies. Volunteer at a soup kitchen or homeless shelter to help serve a meal.

Help a Veteran—Those who have served and sacrificed for our country are all too often forgotten. Remember them this holiday season. A retirement center or local veteran's hospital will be able to give you ideas on how you can best help a veteran. It might be something as simple as spending an hour listening to them share their past experiences or driving them to a doctor's appointment.

Involve the Kids—There are plenty of volunteer opportunities for youngsters, too. Animal shelters are always in need of helping hands. Senior citizens love to have story time with children. Make it a group effort to do something thoughtful for an elderly neighbor. Think of ways you can involve the whole family in a volunteer effort.

Share Your Skills—If you have amazing knitting skills or maybe are excellent at woodworking, think about volunteering to teach a class or lead a workshop at a recreation or senior center. The rewards you'll receive in seeing the joy as others learn something new will far exceed the cost of your time. If you're good at organizing or event planning, any number of organizations could use your assistance.

Think Outside the Box—Volunteers are always needed at shelters (for animals and humans), senior centers, community centers, and hospitals, but a plethora of other opportunities exist. Often holiday parades need volunteers. You can offer to help your local fire department or police station if they hold a holiday charity event. Some communities need help putting up holiday decorations or cleaning up after a community event. Take a look around and you'll find the perfect volunteer opportunity for your talents.

SPREAD CHEER

IF VOLUNTEERING ISN'T YOUR CUP OF TEA, there are still plenty of ways to spread cheer this holiday season!

Thank Volunteers—Even if you aren't able to volunteer, thank those who do. Send a note to your local fire department or a thank-you letter to shelter volunteers.

Manners Matter—In a world where people get into brawls at holiday sales, pursue small acts of kindness. Say thank you to your postal worker. Allow someone to go in front of you at the grocery store. One of my favorite ways to show a little kindness is simply to smile at people. You'll be amazed at what that little bit of cheer can do for others.

Bake Extra—Planning to bake Christmas cookies or other goodies? Make a double batch and drop off a few dozen at a senior center, care home, or homeless shelter.

Buy Extra—If you're already out shopping and enduring the crowds, pick up a toy or two for a child in need. Look for programs like Salvation Army's Angel Tree or a local donation collection center to make sure the gift goes to a needy child.

Travel Assistance—Parking can be a nightmare during the holiday season, especially at points of travel like airports. Give a neighbor or friend a ride to drop them off, or offer to pick someone up.

Share Warmth—Utility costs can skyrocket during cold winter months. If you know someone short on cash or going through a tough time, you can call most utility companies and anonymously pay their gas or electric bill. If they have a fireplace or heat with wood, have a cord of wood delivered anonymously.

Be a Friend—While the holidays are a time brimming with joy for most people, there are those who are lonely and hurting. If you know people who struggle with the season, be sure to include them in a gathering, or even take them to lunch. Let them know they aren't alone or forgotten.

Donate—Numerous charities gladly accept monetary donations, from worldwide organizations to local needs. Do your research, find the one that best matches your beliefs, and look for those that get as much of your donation to the bottom line as possible (like the Justin Cowboy Crisis Fund, which keeps 100 percent of the donations in the fund).

Pen to Paper—There's nothing in the world like a handwritten note from someone you care about. This Christmas, write a heartfelt note or two to friends or loved ones who've made a difference in your life.

Sing-Along—If you don't know a group going caroling, organize one! Just gather friends and family, then make the rounds of your neighborhood or visit an assisted living facility. You'll be amazed by how much people will enjoy hearing your group sing.

PART TWO

RECIPES

APPETIZERS AND BEVERAGES

THE CHRISTMAS SEASON IS THE PERFECT TIME to connect with family and friends. From small, intimate gatherings of less than a dozen to a holiday bash for a hundred, easy-to-make, delicious recipes are an important part of a successful party.

When guests walk in your door, they are filled with eager anticipation, and they're most likely hungry, too!

Offer an assortment of appetizers and beverages that let them know they are welcome and about to be well fed in the warmth and comfort of your home.

Appetizers don't have to be complicated. Even simple recipes, crafted with good, fresh ingredients, can make a huge impact with your guests.

If young ones are attending the party, think about offering beverages that will make them smile.

Get your party started, and off on the right foot, with appetizers and beverages that set the tone for the fun to come.

Bacon-Wrapped Potatoes

There are so many deliciously delightful things you can wrap bacon around, like scallops, shrimp, even water chestnuts.

But living in a house with someone who considers water chestnuts strange and exotic food, I had to find something a little more everyday to encase with bacon.

Baby potatoes are the perfect answer! And they really are so good. Captain Cavedweller described this appetizer best: "It's the perfect combo of smoky, crispy bacon outside and soft, tender spuds inside."

Makes 2 dozen appetizers

3 tablespoons vegetable oil

1 teaspoon all-purpose seasoning

Salt and pepper

24 baby potatoes

12 slices bacon

Preheat oven to 400°F.

Mix oil, seasoning (I like to use Mrs. Dash), and salt and pepper in a bowl. Set aside. Wash the potatoes and pat dry. You can use any variety of baby or fingerling potatoes.

Dip potatoes in oil and seasoning mixture, then place on a parchment-lined baking sheet. Bake for 10 minutes.

Cut bacon strips in half crosswise. Remove potatoes from oven and, using a fork, place potatoes on strips of bacon and roll up. Secure bacon ends with a toothpick and place back on baking sheet.

Bake for 20 to 25 minutes, until bacon is crispy and potatoes are soft.

Serve with ranch dressing or your favorite dip.

Best Bacon Dip

I happened upon this recipe several years ago when I needed an appetizer for a small gathering of friends. After setting the dip on the table with a plate of crackers, I turned around to get something from the refrigerator. By the time I got back to the table, the bowl had nearly been scraped clean!

Needless to say, the dip has gained a popular following among our circle of friends over the years. I've never taken it to a party or potluck and had any leftovers, which is why I always make a little extra to leave at home.

Makes approximately 16 servings

1 cup sour cream

1 cup mayonnaise

1 cup shredded cheese

1 cup chopped tomatoes

1 cup crumbled cooked bacon

In a large mixing bowl, combine all ingredients. You can use your favorite cheese, but my go-to is Colby-Jack for this recipe.

It should be noted that if you use salad dressing instead of good old mayo, your dip will taste weird and the mayo police will take you out and have you horsewhipped.

Just kidding . . . mostly. Use mayonnaise. Pretty please.

The dip can be made a day ahead of time and actually tastes even better when the flavors have time to blend together. Keep refrigerated until ready to serve.

There are a variety of ways you can serve the dip. The first is in a pretty bowl with crackers or crostini bread on the side. Our cracker of choice is Ritz. They taste so good with the dip.

The second option for serving the dip is to core cherry, cocktail, or (my favorite) campari tomatoes, then spoon the dip into the tomatoes and serve. You could also serve it in lettuce cups.

No matter how you present it, this dip is sure to be the hit of any appetizer buffet.

CRANBERRY FETA PINWHEELS

Although I'm the only one at my house who enjoys the creamy tanginess of feta cheese, I love it enough for everyone. These pinwheels are so easy to whip together and can be made a day ahead. Each bite is filled with holiday goodness!

Makes approximately 40 pieces

8 ounces cream cheese, softened

1 cup crumbled feta cheese

1½ cups dried cranberries

½ cup chopped pecans

4 (10-inch) flour tortillas

¼ cup chopped fresh mint

Place softened cream cheese in a mixing bowl and beat until fluffy. Stir in feta cheese, cranberries, and pecans.

Divide the mixture evenly over the four tortillas. To make rolling easier and keep the filling from oozing out, leave a ½-inch border from the edge when you spread out the mixture.

Tightly roll each tortilla and wrap in plastic wrap, making sure ends are tucked in so no air sneaks in to dry out the tortillas.

Refrigerate up to 24 hours before cutting into 1-inch slices. Top with a sprinkling of fresh mint and serve.

MEATBALL BITES

The first time I made these appetizers was a test run before a party. Captain Cavedweller arrived home just as I pulled them out of the oven and devoured half a tray. When he came up for air, he gave me a thumbs-up and said, "They're keepers." Truly, you can't go wrong with these beefy bites.

Makes 2 dozen appetizers

1 sheet refrigerated crescent roll dough

24 meatballs, pre-cooked

1 cup shredded mozzarella cheese

1 teaspoon dried herb seasoning

¼ cup chopped fresh parsley

Barbecue sauce, for serving

Preheat oven to 350°F. Lightly spray a mini muffin tin with nonstick cooking spray.

Unroll dough and cut into twenty-four squares. Place one piece of dough in each muffin cup, pushing dough down so it forms a cup.

Nestle a meatball in each cup and bake for 10 minutes (I use frozen pre-cooked meatballs). While it bakes, mix cheese with dried seasoning. Remove meatballs from oven and top with cheese mixture. Bake an additional 5 to 7 minutes, until cheese is melted and gooey.

Remove from oven, top with chopped parsley, and serve with barbecue sauce on the side or drizzled over the top.

Watermelon Shapes

If you want your youngsters to help with food prep, give them a hands-on project like cutting shapes out of melons. You can use watermelon, cantaloupe, or honeydew. They'll be proud to see their fruit shapes on your appetizer table!

Makes approximately 30 pieces

1 medium seedless watermelon

On a cutting board, cut watermelon into $\frac{1}{2}$- to $\frac{3}{4}$-inch-thick slices.

One slice at a time, place on cutting board and use cookie cutters to cut out shapes. This is a great activity for kids and gets them involved in the food preparations.

If you are planning to leave the rind on for some of the pieces, use a sturdy cookie cutter that can take the pressure necessary to cut through the rind. Give this task to older children.

CHRISTMAS TEA

There's something so comforting about steaming, fragrant tea, especially if it's served in a beautiful cup. When my friends come over for a girls' get-together, I always try to have a pot of spicy tea ready to serve as we get down to our gabfest.

Makes 12 servings

8 cups water

1½ cups granulated sugar

6 tea bags (black unflavored works best)

3 cinnamon sticks

2 tablespoons whole cloves

¼ cup lemon juice

1½ cups orange juice

In a heavy saucepan, bring water to a boil. Add sugar, stirring until dissolved. Add tea bags, cinnamon sticks, and cloves. Simmer, uncovered, for 5 minutes. Strain out spices and remove tea bags. Add juices, stir well to blend, and simmer for an additional minute or two to heat juices.

Serve while hot.

Ombré Punch

When you need a beverage you can serve to all ages that will bring a little awe to your table, try this easy-to-make punch. The trick is to avoid stirring or blending the liquid!

We like it best with orange juice as the base, but you can also use grapefruit juice for a different flavor.

Makes 6 servings

Ice

3 cups orange juice, chilled

Grenadine syrup

Place ice in the bottom of six glasses. Add ½ cup of juice to each glass, then carefully pour 1 teaspoon of grenadine syrup in each glass. That's it! Told you it was easy. Just make sure you do not stir the drink or it will lose the lovely ombré design.

If you prefer to substitute grapefruit juice for orange juice, add a splash of lemon-lime soda to each glass before you add the grenadine syrup.

CRANBERRY PUNCH

The tartness of cranberries pairs so well with the fizziness of sweet soda for a refreshing punch that is hard to beat. Use your favorite cranberry juice or give dark cranberry-pomegranate a try!

Makes 16 servings

1 (2-liter) bottle raspberry soda

Sugar rimmer crystals

1 pomegranate

1 (64-ounce) bottle cranberry-pomegranate juice

½ cup grenadine syrup

Fill two ice cube trays with soda and freeze overnight.

Just before you are ready to serve the punch, pour sugar rimmer crystals onto a dish or a small bowl just big enough for your glasses to fit inside.

Wet the rims of the glasses, one at a time. You can do this with a lemon or lime wedge or plain ol' water. Dip the rims of the glasses into the crystals and set aside.

Cut the pomegranate in half crosswise. Hold the pomegranate, cut side down, over a medium bowl and hit the back with a spoon to release the seeds (or you can cheat and buy a package of pomegranate seeds at the grocery store). Rinse and drain. Drop a scattering of seeds in each glass.

Place the ice in your punch bowl, pour in cranberry juice, grenadine syrup, and the remainder of the soda. Stir to mix. Ladle into glasses and watch your guests turn into glass-licking lunatics as they try to get every last little speck of the rimmer off their glasses and dig each little seed out of their glass.

TO MAKE SUGAR RIMMER CRYSTALS

To make sugar to rim the glasses, you can either infuse it (see page 74 for details) or simply place ½ cup coarse sugar in a resealable bag, then add a few drops of food coloring and a tablespoon of flavoring (found in the baking aisle). Squeeze the air out of the bag, close, and knead until the flavoring and color are mixed with the sugar. Spread the sugar out on a piece of parchment to dry, then use to rim glasses.

If you use cranberry-strawberry juice, for example, flavor the sugar with strawberry flavoring.

Reindeer Fizz

A few years ago, Captain Cavedweller and I were in Atlanta for a conference. The Coca-Cola headquarters was just down the street from the hotel where we were staying, so we ventured there one morning. Two hours later, while sampling our way through dozens of soda flavors, we both came to a stop after tasting Barq's Red Crème Soda. It's almost impossible to describe the exact flavor beyond "crimson deliciousness." If you think a root beer float is yummy, wait until you give this recipe a whirl.

Makes 2 servings

1 cup vanilla ice cream

1 can Barq's Red Crème Soda

Whipped cream

Sprinkles

Scoop ½ cup ice cream into a glass, then pour in half a can of the soda. Once it stops threatening to fizz over the top of the glass, add a generous dollop of whipped cream and top with sprinkles. Add a colorful holiday straw and enjoy!

Note: *If your local stores don't carry Barq's Red Crème Soda, you can find it online. I've ordered it from Amazon and have also found it at the Soda Emporium.*

BREAKFASTS AND BREADS

WITH BUSY SCHEDULES, A BIG FAMILY breakfast doesn't happen often at our house, but when it does, we try to make it special with delicious dishes and special treats. Whether you're looking for something quick and easy or have time to make something memorable, these recipes are sure to get your day off to a grand start.

Banana Bread

Both Captain Cavedweller and I love most anything banana flavored. I first discovered this recipe in a cookbook I received as a wedding shower gift. It's always moist and packed with that banana taste we adore.

Makes 1 loaf

1¾ cups all-purpose flour, divided

⅔ cup granulated sugar

2 teaspoons baking powder

½ teaspoon baking soda

¼ teaspoon salt

2–3 (1½ cups mashed) ripe bananas

⅓ cup butter or shortening

2 tablespoons milk

1 teaspoon vanilla extract

2 eggs

1 teaspoon cinnamon

½ cup chopped walnuts

Preheat oven to 350°F. Grease and flour a standard-size bread pan.

In a mixing bowl, combine 1 cup flour, sugar, baking powder, baking soda, and salt. Mash two to three ripe (or overripe; the riper the banana the stronger the flavor) bananas to make 1½ cups. Add bananas, butter, milk, and vanilla to dry ingredients. Mix on low until blended, then beat on high for 2 minutes. Add eggs and remaining flour; beat until blended. Stir in cinnamon and nuts.

Bake for 55 to 60 minutes, until golden brown and starting to pull away from the edges of the pan.

Eggnog Doughnuts

I've never been a big fan of eggnog until I tried these easy doughnuts. Talk about tasty! They are wonderful and have a holiday flavor that can't be beat.

Makes approximately 6 doughnuts

1 cup all-purpose flour

1 teaspoon baking powder

¼ teaspoon sea salt

¼ cup granulated sugar

2 tablespoons butter, softened

1 large egg

½ cup eggnog

GLAZE

½ cup powdered sugar

2 tablespoons eggnog

Grated nutmeg

Preheat oven to 325°F. Generously spray doughnut pan with nonstick spray. (If you don't have a doughnut pan, you can use mini bundt pans, too.)

Mix the flour, baking powder, and salt. Set aside.

Cream sugar and butter. Add egg and eggnog. Mix well. Gradually add dry ingredients, mixing until well blended.

Split the batter evenly between each mold. Bake for 10 to 13 minutes, until dough is set. Transfer to cooling rack. Glaze once cooled.

To make the glaze, mix powdered sugar and eggnog until smooth. Dip doughnuts into glaze and return to rack. Sprinkle nutmeg over the top.

GRANNY'S CINNAMON ROLLS

Sue McKinnon, mom of Nick LaDuke, shared this recipe she learned from her mother-in-law. Nick's story starts on page 63.

Makes approximately 24 rolls

1 cup milk, scalded

2 tablespoons shortening

1 package Rapid Rise yeast

½ cup granulated sugar, divided

4½ cups all-purpose flour (approximately— depends on the moisture in the air), divided

1 teaspoon salt

1 teaspoon vanilla extract

1 egg

3 tablespoons butter, melted

Ground cinnamon

Granulated sugar

Nuts or raisins, optional

To scald, pour milk into a heavy-bottomed saucepan and heat on medium-low for 4 to 5 minutes, until milk steams and starts to bubble. Stir with a wooden or silicone spoon (metal may react with the proteins in the milk). Do not let mixture boil. Pour scalded milk into a large bowl. Melt shortening in scalded milk, stirring well to combine.

While milk is cooling, proof the yeast. In a medium-sized bowl, dissolve yeast in ½ cup lukewarm water. When it is dissolved, stir in ½ cup flour (taken from the 4½ cups of flour) and 3 tablespoons sugar (taken from the ½ cup of sugar). Let proof at a lukewarm, even temperature until mixture becomes bubbly (approximately 20 minutes).

Add proofed yeast to cooled milk (milk should not feel cold to touch; you should not feel any temperature difference).

Add salt, vanilla, egg, and the remaining sugar.

Beat in flour (beat half the flour amount in the bowl, then turn out on a floured surface). Work as much flour into the dough as it takes to make it not sticky.

Knead bread dough until it can roll off a surface without sticking. Remember, kneading is what makes an even texture. Don't worry about over-kneading, just don't overdo the amount of flour.

Grease a large pan or bowl (one you have a lid for). Put the dough in the container, rub into the grease, and flip the dough over so the greased side is facing up. Cover the container. Set in a warm, even-temperature area. The dough should double in approximately 1 hour.

Turn raised dough onto a lightly floured surface. Flatten dough into a rectangle with a rolling pin. Spread melted butter over the entire flattened area, then cover with cinnamon and sugar to taste. Optionally, add walnuts, pecans, or raisins. Roll dough lengthwise into a log and slice in 1-inch slices. Place in a greased cake pan.

Let cinnamon rolls rise to double in size (approximately 45 minutes).

Bake in a preheated 375°F-oven for 15 to 20 minutes.

Ham and Egg Breakfast Cups

Captain Cavedweller and I were out of town and decided to try a restaurant that looked promising. We enjoyed a hearty breakfast casserole that was superb. When we returned home, I attempted to re-create it. Eventually, I got it right. The casserole takes a while to bake, so for those mornings when we're in a rush or on the go, these breakfast cups using the same ingredients are perfect.

Makes approximately 12 servings

1 ham steak, cubed

4 eggs, beaten

4 cups shredded hash browns

½ cup heavy cream

1 cup shredded Colby-Jack cheese

Salt and pepper

1 teaspoon all-purpose seasoning (like Mrs. Dash)

Additional ½ cup cheese, optional

Preheat oven to 400°F. Spray the wells of a muffin tin with nonstick spray.

Mix ham, eggs, hash browns, cream, cheese, and seasoning until well blended and spoon into muffin tin wells.

Bake for 18 to 20 minutes, until brown around the edges. If desired, sprinkle on more cheese and bake an additional 5 minutes.

Overnight French Toast

One of the best things about this French toast (other than the fact it is creamy deliciousness with a hint of maple) is that it can be assembled the day before, which makes it perfect for a Christmas brunch when you don't want to be tied to the kitchen for long. Just place it in a cold oven, bake, and enjoy the silky custard-like filling with a crispy crust.

Makes approximately 6 servings

½ cup butter

¾ cup brown sugar, packed

2 tablespoons maple syrup

6 slices French bread

4 large eggs

½ cup heavy cream

½ cup milk

1 tablespoon vanilla extract

¼ teaspoon salt

Melt butter in a microwave-safe bowl. Stir in sugar and syrup, heating in 30-second intervals until sugar dissolves.

Grease a 9 x 13-inch baking dish. Spoon the brown sugar mixture into bottom of pan.

Cut bread into 1-inch cubes and spread across sugar mixture.

Whisk together eggs, cream, milk, vanilla, and salt. Pour over bread. Cover pan with plastic wrap and refrigerate overnight.

When ready to bake, remove plastic wrap and place pan in a cold oven. Bake at 350°F for 30 to 40 minutes, until top is light brown and syrup is bubbling. Serve with fresh berries, whipped cream, or a dusting of powdered sugar if desired.

Raspberry Cream Cheese Rolls

These unbelievably soft, decadent rolls come from my standard cinnamon roll recipe. One day, I got to thinking about ingredients I could use beyond cinnamon, sugar, and butter—and these yummy gems were the result.

Makes approximately 24 rolls

DOUGH

2 cups milk

½ cup vegetable oil

½ cup granulated sugar

1 package active dry yeast

4½ cups all-purpose flour, divided

½ teaspoon baking powder

½ teaspoon baking soda

1 teaspoon salt

FILLING

4 ounces cream cheese

2 tablespoons butter

¼ cup granulated sugar

1 teaspoon vanilla extract

2½ cups frozen raspberries

½ tablespoon cornstarch

2 tablespoons butter, melted (to grease pan)

CREAM CHEESE FROSTING

4 ounces cream cheese

¼ cup butter

1 teaspoon vanilla extract

2 cups powdered sugar

Heat the milk, oil, and sugar in a large saucepan over medium heat. Do not allow it to boil, but simmer until hot. Set aside and cool until lukewarm (think baby bottle temperature). Sprinkle the yeast over the top and let sit on the milk for 1 minute, then stir to dissolve yeast.

Add 4 cups of the flour and stir until just combined. Cover with a clean kitchen towel (flour sack towels work best) and set aside in a warm place for 1 hour. (I often set my bread to rise in front of the fireplace.)

While dough is rising, bring cream cheese and butter to room temperature. Make the filling by combining 4 ounces cream cheese, 2 tablespoons butter, sugar, and vanilla extract, stirring until smooth. In a separate bowl, toss frozen berries with cornstarch. Let rest for approximately 10 minutes.

Once the dough has risen, remove the towel and add the baking powder, baking soda, salt, and remaining $\frac{1}{2}$ cup flour. Stir to combine.

Roll the dough onto a floured baking surface into approximately a 30 x 10-inch rectangle. Spread cream cheese mixture evenly over the dough, then sprinkle with berries.

Beginning at the long end farthest from you, roll the rectangle tightly toward you. Use both hands and work slowly (or coerce someone to help you with promises of tasty baked goods). Be careful to keep the roll tight. It's okay if the filling oozes out a little. When you reach the end, pinch the seam together. Transfer to a cutting board and make $1\frac{1}{2}$-inch slices.

Grease baking pan(s) with melted butter, then place the sliced rolls in the pan, careful not to crowd them too close together.

Preheat the oven to 375°F. Cover the pan(s) with a towel and set to rise on the countertop for 20 minutes before baking. Remove the towel and bake for 13 to 15 minutes, until tops are lightly browned. Do not let rolls get overly brown or they will be tough.

While the rolls are baking, make the icing by mixing 4 ounces cream cheese, $\frac{1}{4}$ cup butter, and vanilla with powdered sugar until smooth.

Remove rolls from the oven. While they are still warm, drizzle with frosting. As the rolls sit, they absorb the sweet frosting, which makes them even more delicious.

Note: *Bake in disposable foil pans for gift giving, or hide them in the freezer for when you need a delicious treat!*

Swedish Pancakes

This recipe comes from Shana Bailey. Her paternal grandmother made them and then taught Shana's mother to make them. Shana said her mom comes over on Christmas morning to make these special pancakes for the family. What a wonderful tradition!

Makes 12 pancakes

3 eggs

3 tablespoons granulated sugar

2 cups milk

½ teaspoon salt

1 cup all-purpose flour

3 tablespoons bacon drippings

In a medium bowl, beat eggs. Add sugar, milk, salt, and flour. Add bacon drippings and mix together.

Coat frying pan with butter or oil and set on medium heat. Add about ⅓ cup batter and swirl the pan to coat the bottom with batter. Cook until the pancake sets, about 1 to 1½ minutes. Using a rubber spatula, carefully lift the pancake by the edges and flip. Cook until it is lightly golden, about 30 seconds.

Transfer to a pie plate in a warm oven. Repeat with the remaining batter.

To serve, top with fresh strawberries or syrup.

SOUPS AND SALADS

AFTER A DAY OF SLEDDING OR AN EVENING OF CAROLING, there's nothing quite like a bowl of hot soup to warm you from the inside out. Soup is a popular dinner go-to at our house on cold winter days. Accompany the soup with the bright taste of a salad made from the freshest ingredients available.

Chicken Dumpling Soup

This soup adds a little spin to classic chicken and dumplings. Filled with soft dumplings, tender chicken, and veggies, it's perfect to chase away a chill while indulging in a little comfort food.

Makes 6 servings

4 cups chicken broth

6 cups water

1 cup sliced celery

1½ cups cooked potatoes, cut into chunks

1 bag frozen mixed veggies

3 cups cooked chicken, cut into bite-sized pieces

1 teaspoon chopped fresh parsley

½ teaspoon onion flakes

Salt and pepper

1 can refrigerator biscuits (*do not* use the flaky variety!)

2 cans cream of chicken soup

In a stockpot, mix the chicken broth with water, then add celery, potatoes, frozen veggies, chicken, parsley, onion flakes, and salt and pepper to taste. Bring to a boil on medium heat.

Add the refrigerator biscuits by pinching off a quarter-sized piece at a time and dropping into the pot. Cover and simmer without peeking into the pot for about 15 minutes or until the biscuit dough is nearly cooked.

Add the cream of chicken soup and gently stir to mix. Let simmer for 5 minutes and serve.

Bunkhouse Stew

When I was growing up, we often had stew. The ingredients varied, but what remained consistent was that my youngest niece did not like to eat it. My dad started giving the stew funny names like Rainbow Stew and Gopher Stew to try to get her to eat it. Sometimes it even worked!

Makes approximately 8 servings

3 cups water

1 can beef broth

½ cup baby carrots

1 (15-ounce) can whole kernel corn

1 (26-ounce) can Ranch Style beans

4 medium potatoes, peeled and cubed

1 cup barley

1 tablespoon chili powder

¼ teaspoon sugar

Salt and pepper

2 pounds ground beef

1 medium onion (yellow or white)

1 teaspoon minced garlic

¾ cup chopped celery

In a large stockpot, combine water and broth with carrots, corn, beans, potatoes, and barley as well as chili powder, sugar, and salt and pepper to taste. Bring to a boil, stirring occasionally.

While it's cooking, brown beef, drain, and then add onion, garlic, and celery. Cook until soft.

Add beef mixture to stockpot. Reduce heat, cover, and simmer for at least 20 minutes, until potatoes are tender.

Oyster Stew

Renee and Hank Moss have many holiday traditions they observe every year. After an evening of caroling on Christmas Eve, they return home to enjoy Oyster Stew by candlelight, a tradition started by Renee's grandparents many years ago. This recipe is simple and fast to make.

Makes approximately 4 servings

½ cup butter

3–4 cups milk

2 (3.75-ounce) cans stewed oysters

Salt and pepper

Melt butter in a large skillet. Slowly add enough milk to fill the skillet. Add the stewed oysters, salt, and pepper. Heat through, about 10 minutes, stirring occasionally.

Serve with oyster crackers.

Caprese Salad

This salad is a breeze to make, full of bright colors and fresh flavors. It's perfect to add to a sit-down dinner or buffet!

Makes 6 servings

1 package grape or cherry tomatoes

Fresh spinach leaves

Balsamic vinegar

1 package marinated mozzarella balls

Sea salt and chopped fresh parsley, optional

Rinse tomatoes and spinach leaves and gently pat dry.

On a large serving platter, layer spinach leaves, forming a circle around the edge and working your way in. In the center of the platter, set a small bowl and fill it with balsamic vinegar. Place tomatoes and mozzarella balls around the bowl.

If desired, sprinkle with sea salt and freshly diced parsley. Serve immediately.

Cowboy Pasta Salad

I was in college before I realized you could buy dried pasta in a box and enjoy it anytime you want. My mom always made her own, which is probably why I love homemade noodles! This pasta salad can be served as a side dish or could also do duty as a main entree.

Makes 10–12 servings

1 pound dried mini pasta shells

½ teaspoon olive oil

1 pound bacon

1 pound lean ground beef

Salt and pepper

1 cup mayonnaise

⅓ cup barbecue sauce

2 tablespoons Worcestershire sauce

1 (15-ounce) can whole kernel sweet corn, drained

2 cups cherry tomatoes, halved

1½ cups shredded Colby-Jack cheese

½ cup diced chives

Pinch of red pepper flakes, optional

2½ teaspoons hot chili sauce, optional

Bring a large pot of water to boil. Add pasta and cook until al dente, according to package directions. Drain and rinse under cold water. Drizzle with olive oil and stir to prevent sticking.

Saute bacon over medium heat until crispy, about 10 minutes. Transfer to a paper towel–lined plate to drain grease, then crumble. Leave a little bacon grease in the skillet and brown ground beef, cooking until no longer pink. Season with salt and pepper and set aside.

In a large bowl, whisk together mayonnaise, barbecue sauce, and Worcestershire sauce until smooth. (For added kick, stir in optional red pepper flakes and hot chili sauce.) Add cooked pasta, bacon, beef, corn, tomatoes, cheese, and chives. Toss to coat, and serve.

WEDGE SALAD

This salad, made with iceberg lettuce and a flavorful dressing, has become a favorite at our house (it's probably because of the bacon!).

Makes 4 servings

½ cup sour cream

½ cup buttermilk

¼ cup mayonnaise

1 teaspoon garlic salt

¼ teaspoon pepper

1½ teaspoons dried dill

2 teaspoons lemon juice

2 dashes hot sauce, optional

1 head iceberg lettuce

4 slices bacon, cooked and crumbled

½ cup shredded cheddar cheese

In a small bowl, combine sour cream, buttermilk, mayonnaise, garlic salt, pepper, dill, and lemon juice (and hot sauce if desired). Stir well and set aside.

Wash lettuce and remove outer leaves, then cut into quarters. Place wedges on individual plates or a platter.

Drizzle with dressing, then sprinkle with bacon and cheese. Serve immediately.

Winter Fruit Salad

Use the best in-season produce to make this vibrant salad. It looks gorgeous on a table and is full of delicious bites of sweet fruit, too!

Makes approximately 6 servings

½ cup pomegranate seeds

1 red apple, cored and chopped

1 green apple, cored and chopped

2 pears, cored and chopped

1 cup mandarin orange slices

3 kiwis, peeled and sliced

2 tablespoons lime juice

2 tablespoons honey

Cut the pomegranate in half crosswise. Hold the pomegranate, cut side down, over a medium bowl and hit the back with a spoon to release the seeds. Rinse and drain. (Or cheat like I sometimes do and buy the pomegranate seeds already removed and in a neat little container.)

Gently mix all the fruit together in a large bowl.

In a liquid measuring cup, combine the lime juice and honey, stirring until incorporated.

Drizzle the dressing over fruit and toss to coat. Serve chilled.

SIDE DISHES

SIDE DISHES ARE AN OFTEN OVERLOOKED but important part of every meal, especially when the flavors and textures complement the main course to perfection.

Experiment with some new dishes and add a little flair the next time you sit down at the dinner table. Even standard potatoes can get a new look and taste with a little inspiration.

Cheesy Broccoli Bites

An old broccoli and cheese casserole classic gets updated in these easy-to-make bites!

Makes 24 bites

1 large bunch broccoli florets

¼ cup water

½ cup panko crumbs

2 eggs, lightly beaten

¼ cup grated onion

¼ cup mayonnaise

¼ cup sour cream

1 cup grated cheddar cheese

1 teaspoon lemon juice

½ teaspoon kosher salt

Steam broccoli florets in a microwave-safe bowl with ¼ cup of water for 4 to 5 minutes, until tender. Rinse with cold water to stop cooking process. Drain water. Chop to fill 2½ cups. Lightly press on broccoli with the back of a spoon, then drain excess liquid.

Preheat oven to 350°F.

Mix crumbs and beaten eggs together. Add onion, mayonnaise, sour cream, cheese, lemon juice, and salt. Stir in broccoli.

Coat a muffin tin with nonstick spray. Distribute broccoli mixture in the wells of the tin.

Bake for 25 minutes, until lightly browned on top. Serve immediately.

CRISPY RANCH POTATOES

If you enjoy a good spud, these potatoes are buttery, flavorful, and absolutely yummy. They pair well with many main dishes, but are also good enough to eat all on their own.

Makes 6–8 servings

3 tablespoons butter, melted

3 tablespoons olive oil

10–12 russet potatoes, peeled

Salt

2 tablespoons powdered ranch dressing mix

5 slices bacon

Fresh thyme sprigs

Chopped parsley, optional

Preheat oven to 375°F.

Combine the melted butter and oil in a small dish. Set aside. Brush a round 9- or 10-inch baking dish with a little of the butter and oil mixture. Thinly slice the potatoes, keeping each potato together as you slice. Arrange potatoes in the baking dish. Sprinkle with salt and ranch dressing mix. Drizzle with remaining butter and oil mixture.

Bake for 1 hour and 25 minutes. Cover the pan loosely with foil during the first 30 minutes of baking. Remove from oven and baste potatoes with butter and oil from the bottom of the dish. Return to oven without the foil for the remaining 55 minutes.

While the potatoes are baking, fry bacon in a small pan until crispy. Remove from the pan, drain on a paper towel, then crumble. Remove potatoes from oven and sprinkle bacon over the top. For a nice finish, wash sprigs of thyme and place on top of potatoes.

Bake for an additional 35 minutes. Remove from oven and discard thyme sprigs. Add another dash of salt and chopped parsley if desired, and serve immediately.

Green Bean Bacon Bundles

We've always been fans of green beans simmered with bits of bacon, but these bundles . . . oh my gracious! They take that delicious bacon flavor to a whole new level. These are beautiful on their own or placed around your main dish for an added element of visual appeal.

Makes 4–6 servings

6–8 slices bacon

1½ pounds fresh green beans

½ teaspoon baking soda

Salt and pepper

1 tablespoon maple syrup

Preheat oven to 375°F. Line a baking sheet with parchment paper.

Cut bacon strips in half so you have twelve to sixteen pieces. Place on baking sheet and cook in the oven for about 10 minutes. You don't want the bacon fully cooked, but on its way there.

Trim and wash green beans. Bring a large pot of water to a boil. Add baking soda, which helps the beans retain their glorious bright green color. Add green beans and cook for 3 minutes. Drain beans and place in a bowl of ice water to stop cooking.

Dab beans dry. Remove bacon from oven and the baking sheet, then set aside. Toss green beans on baking sheet to cover with all those wonderful bacon drippings. Add salt and pepper to taste.

Bundle six to eight green beans, wrap with a bacon strip, and secure with a toothpick. Return to the parchment-lined baking sheet. Repeat with remaining green beans and bacon.

Drizzle maple syrup over the bundles.

Roast for 20 minutes or until bacon is crisp.

Hatch Green Chilies Squash Casserole

There's nothing quite like the flavors of home to take you back to happy times and memories. Tona Andrade, a barrel racer and rancher, shares this colorful and filling side dish that comes from her roots in New Mexico.

Makes approximately 8 servings

4–5 medium summer squash

1 medium onion, diced

1 tablespoon butter

1 cup peeled and roasted green chilies

1 egg, slightly beaten

1 cup crushed saltine crackers

2 cups grated cheddar cheese

1 (15-ounce) can whole kernel corn, optional

Salt and garlic salt

Preheat oven to 350°F.

Slice squash in 1- to 1½-inch slices and parboil (precook) in a small amount of water until tender. Mash squash and set aside.

Saute onion in butter until soft and then combine with squash, chiles, egg, crackers, cheese, corn (if you're using it), and salt and garlic salt to taste. Pour into a 2-quart casserole dish.

Bake for approximately 30 minutes. Remove from oven and serve immediately.

Parmesan Cauliflower Steak

If you love cauliflower, this side dish will make your taste buds celebrate. Even if you view cauliflower as a stinky, rather dull vegetable, give this a try. I promise it's far, far different from that mushy, smelly stuff so often associated with cauliflower.

Makes 3–4 servings

1 head cauliflower

Salt

2 tablespoons olive oil

⅓ cup freshly grated Parmesan cheese

Preheat oven to 425°F.

Wash head of cauliflower, then cut into 1-inch-thick slices. Sprinkle with salt.

In a large cast-iron or oven-safe skillet, heat olive oil. Add cauliflower slices to hot skillet and sear for approximately 3 minutes on one side, then turn over and cook for 1 minute.

Slide the pan into the oven and roast for 10 to 15 minutes, until stem is tender. Sprinkle tops with Parmesan cheese and return to oven for another 5 minutes.

Remove from oven and serve.

MAIN DISHES

IF YOUR HOUSE IS LIKE OURS, THERE'S NOT ALWAYS TIME to create a grand main course. In fact, sometimes we're doing good just to get a hot meal on the table.

But there's something so comforting and nourishing about sitting down over a meal and sharing about the day.

Whether you're serving a quick one-skillet meal before rushing back out the door to one of the dozens of events filling your calendar, or lingering around the table after dining on a culinary feast, season everything you prepare with a dash of caring affection.

It will add to the flavor of the dish and enrich your life right along with your heart.

Beefy Gnocchi

The first time I made gnocchi, I didn't pay attention to the recommended cooking time, got distracted, and came back fifteen minutes later to find a pan filled with a gooey, gluey mass that did not even taste as good as old-fashioned school paste. Determined to try again, I made sure I cooked it exactly as the directions specified. It was so good, and turned me into a fan. This easy dish features skillet gnocchi topped with some favorites the hungry men in your life will appreciate!

Makes 4–5 servings

BRISKET

1 sweet onion, sliced

1–2 tablespoons meat spice rub

2–3 pounds brisket

2 cups barbecue sauce

2 cups apple cider

2 tablespoons liquid smoke

GNOCCHI

3 tablespoons butter

2 (12-ounce) packages skillet gnocchi

1 (15-ounce) can Ranch Style beans

1 cup shredded Colby-Jack cheese

½ cup sour cream

Spray the inside of a slow cooker with nonstick cooking spray, or (my preference) line with a disposable liner. Place onions in bottom of slow cooker. Pat spice rub into brisket, then place on top of onions.

In a bowl, whisk together barbecue sauce, apple cider, and liquid smoke. Pour over brisket.

Cover and cook on low for 10 hours.

Remove brisket to a cutting board and allow to rest about 10 minutes. Thinly slice the meat against the grain.

Melt butter in a large skillet. Add gnocchi and cook on medium-high for about 5 minutes, continuously stirring to make sure gnocchi is spread out and cooking evenly.

Heat beans according to package directions.

On a platter or individual plates, layer gnocchi with meat, beans, onions cooked with the brisket, cheese, and sour cream. Top it off with a dollop of sauce scooped from the juices simmering in the slow cooker.

Carla's Chicken Casserole

This recipe comes from auctioneer Carla Harrison, wife of rodeo barrelman John Harrison, and is a tasty combination that will have even your pickiest eater asking for a second helping!

Makes approximately 10 servings

2–3 boneless, skinless chicken breasts

2 tablespoons butter

3 tablespoons white wine

1 family-sized box Chicken Rice-A-Roni

½ white onion, chopped

3–4 stalks celery, chopped

2 cups sour cream

Salt and pepper

1–2 cups shredded cheddar cheese

Preheat oven to 350°F.

Place chicken breasts in a casserole dish and top with butter and wine. Bake for 1 hour, until juices run clear. Remove from oven and either shred or cube.

While the chicken is cooking, prepare Rice-A-Roni according to package directions.

In a large bowl, combine chicken, rice, onions, celery, sour cream, salt, and pepper.

Spoon into a large greased casserole dish and cover with shredded cheese.

Bake for 20 minutes, until cheese is melted. Remove from oven and serve.

Meatloaf with Leroy's Gravy

Meatloaf used to be something we avoided at our house. Captain Cavedweller was never a fan, and I'm allergic to processed tomatoes, so that pretty well eliminated every recipe I had. One afternoon, as I pulled a package of ground beef out of the freezer, I decided to see if I could find or create a recipe for meatloaf that didn't use ketchup or any kind of canned tomato product. That turned out to be a fabulous decision. After finding a few recipes online, I combined the elements I liked most from each one and developed a meatloaf recipe that is far from traditional, but tasty all the same. Pair it with Leroy's gravy (named after CC's favorite Christmas song. Seriously, wouldn't a redneck reindeer love a helping of yummy gravy?) and you have a meal full of old-fashioned comfort and delicious flavor.

Makes 6–8 servings

MEATLOAF

3 stalks celery

¼ cup chopped fresh onion

1 tablespoon olive oil

1½–2 pounds ground beef

3 eggs

⅔ cup milk

1 tablespoon parsley

1½ cups panko crumbs

1 teaspoon all-purpose seasoning

Dash of salt

GRAVY

4 tablespoons meat drippings

3 tablespoons butter, divided

4 tablespoons all-purpose flour

2 cups beef broth (chicken works, too)

Preheat oven to 350°F. Line a rimmed baking pan with foil or parchment paper and spray with nonstick spray.

Wash celery then thinly slice. If using fresh onion, chop it into fine pieces.

Heat olive oil in a small skillet on medium heat and add celery and onion. Cook until celery is softened, stirring frequently. Remove from heat.

While celery cools slightly, mix ground beef with eggs, milk, parsley, panko crumbs, seasoning, and salt. Add celery and mix until thoroughly blended.

Form a loaf in the baking pan that is about 12 inches long by 4 to 5 inches wide by 1½ to 2 inches deep.

Bake for 1 hour, until the outside is a nice, deep brown. Remove from the oven.

To make the gravy, scrape up 4 tablespoons of meat drippings (or, if you have bacon drippings, that will work, too). While meatloaf rests, add meat drippings to skillet. Over medium heat, melt 2 tablespoons of the butter with drippings then add flour, stirring constantly until flour reaches a gorgeous golden-brown color. Add broth and simmer until gravy has thickened, stirring occasionally to keep it from sticking.

Just before serving, add remaining 1 tablespoon butter, stirring to blend.

PRIME RIB

During the early years of our marriage, when eating out was an extravagance we saved for, Captain Cavedweller and I would, on rare occasions, splurge and order prime rib. There was just nothing like that rich, tender meat encased in a crisp, tantalizing crust. Since neither one of us are excited about eating turkey for two major holidays in a row, we decided to try making prime rib for Christmas one year. Nervous that we'd somehow mess up this expensive cut of beef, we researched, read directions, took advice from others, and ended up cooking a wonderful piece of meat. It's not hard at all to make good prime rib. Plan on about a pound of meat per person.

Makes 4–6 servings

1 (4–5 pound) beef rib roast

Seasoning or meat rub

Coarse salt

The day before you cook the prime rib, rub it with your seasoning of choice and give it a good coating of salt. I like to use coarse sea salt. By doing this the day before you cook the meat, the salt has a chance to melt into the surface and penetrate into the roast, helping to hold in moisture.

Allow the roast to air-dry, uncovered, on a rack set over a rimmed baking sheet or pan in the fridge overnight.

Preheat oven to 250°F.

Place roast, with fat cap up, on a V-rack set in a large roasting pan or on a wire rack set in a rimmed baking sheet. Place in oven and cook until center of roast registers 120–125°F on an instant-read thermometer for rare, 130°F for medium-rare, or 135°F for medium to medium-well. This will take approximately 3½ to 4 hours for a 5-pound roast.

Remove roast from oven and tent loosely with foil. Allow meat to rest for about 30 minutes.

Kick the oven temperature up to 500°F.

Remove foil and return roast to the oven for about 6 to 8 minutes, until the outside is crispy and browned. Remove the roast from the oven, carve, and serve immediately.

Roasted Chicken

We enjoy a good roasted chicken at our house, but it took awhile to find the perfect recipe. I want my meat moist and tender. Captain Cavedweller is more focused on how crispy the skin gets. Then I discovered that by removing the spine through the spatchcock (now there's a ten dollar word for you) or butterfly method and cooking the chicken at a high temperature, we can get the best of both worlds—crispy chicken with tender, moist meat. Surround it with your favorite veggies for an easy meal in one pan.

Makes approximately 6 servings

1 large chicken

2 tablespoons olive oil

1 tablespoon salt

1 teaspoon baking powder

2 teaspoons parsley (fresh or dried)

1½–2 pounds baby potatoes

3 celery stalks, chopped

1 cup sweet baby carrots

1 medium onion, chopped

Preheat oven to 500°F.

Using sharp kitchen shears, remove spine from chicken. Flatten chicken by placing skin side up on a cutting board and applying firm pressure to the breastbone. You've successfully just spatchcocked your chicken. Congratulations!

Set the chicken on a wire rack inside a foil-lined, rimmed baking sheet. Position the chicken so the breasts are aligned in the center of the baking sheet and the legs are close to the edge. The legs need to get as much heat as possible to cook faster while the breast cooks slower in the middle, retaining moisture.

Drizzle oil over the chicken. Combine salt with baking powder and parsley. Sprinkle all over chicken and rub to distribute evenly over skin. Arrange potatoes, celery, carrots, and onion around chicken.

Roast chicken until thickest part of breast close to the bone registers 150°F, about 45 minutes. If the chicken starts to darken too quickly, reduce temperature to 450°F.

Remove chicken from oven, transfer to cutting board, tent loosely with foil, and allow to rest 5 minutes before carving. Serve with roasted vegetables.

Wild Rice Sausage Skillet

On those nights when you don't have a lot of time but still want something hot and filling, being able to make dinner in one skillet sure comes in handy. You can make this with either sausage or chicken. You can also add whatever veggies you like.

Makes 6–8 servings

1 cup wild rice

2 cups chicken broth

1½ pounds fully cooked smoked beef sausage, sliced

2 cups broccoli

1 red pepper, sliced

1 zucchini, sliced

1 can water chestnuts, sliced

1 can cream of mushroom soup

1 cup shredded Colby-Jack cheese

Cook wild rice according to package directions, replacing 2 cups of water with chicken broth in a deep, heavy skillet.

When it's finished cooking, add sausage and vegetables. Cover and simmer for about 6 minutes, until the veggies are tender and the sausage is hot. Stir in mushroom soup and simmer an additional minute or two until hot, then remove from heat.

Top with cheese and serve.

COOKIES

THERE'S JUST SOMETHING NOSTALGIC AND WONDERFUL about cookies that takes me right back to my childhood years. That, and I love the sweet goodness of a cookie! Cookies are perfect for giving as gifts, greeting friends, sharing with family, and enjoying by the fire with a cup of hot chocolate on a cold, wintery day. Since cookies come in all shapes, sizes, and flavors, there's sure to be one everybody will enjoy.

CANDY CANE SNOWBALLS

Whether you call them Mexican Wedding Cakes, Russian Tea Cakes, or Mothballs, these delicious, buttery cookies are always a hit. Hide a Hershey's Candy Cane Kiss inside for a special holiday surprise!

Makes 24 cookies

1 cup butter, softened

1 cup powdered sugar, divided

1 teaspoon vanilla extract

2¼ cups all-purpose flour

¼ teaspoon salt

1 bag Hershey's Candy Cane Kisses

Preheat oven to 400°F.

Mix butter, ½ cup powdered sugar, and vanilla in a large bowl. Stir in flour and salt until dough sticks together.

Unwrap Candy Cane Kisses and mold dough around each kiss, placing cookies an inch or two apart on an ungreased baking sheet.

Bake for 6 to 8 minutes, until set but not brown. Remove from cookie sheet. Cool slightly on a wire rack. While still warm, roll cookies in remaining powdered sugar. Cool on wire rack completely. Roll in powdered sugar again.

If desired, crush a peppermint stick and roll tops of cookies in the candy for added flair.

Chewy Choco Bars

The first time I made these cookies, I thought my taste buds might begin a happy dance. They are moist, chewy, chocolate perfection with a hint of coconut. The bars are easy to package for gift-giving, or enjoy them at home.

Makes 24–30 bars

1½ cups semi-sweet chocolate chips

1 (14-ounce) can sweetened condensed milk

2 tablespoons butter, plus 1 cup butter, melted

2¼ cups light brown sugar

2 eggs

2 cups all-purpose flour

½ cup chopped macadamia nuts

1 cup flaked coconut

1 teaspoon salt

1 teaspoon vanilla extract

Preheat oven to 350°F.

In a microwave-safe bowl, combine the chocolate chips, sweetened condensed milk, and 2 tablespoons of the butter. Microwave on high for 1 minute. Stir, then heat for another minute in 30-second intervals, making sure chips are melted. Set aside.

In a large bowl, blend remaining melted butter with brown sugar and eggs on medium speed. Add flour, nuts, coconut, salt, and vanilla extract and mix until thoroughly combined.

Spread approximately half the dough on an ungreased 10 x 15-inch jelly roll pan. Drizzle the chocolate mixture over the dough, then drop small spoonfuls of the remaining dough on top of the chocolate. Drag the tip of a knife through the dough and chocolate to create a swirl pattern.

Bake for 25 minutes, until the top is lightly browned. Let cool for 15 minutes. Cut into bars.

Gingerbread Bars

I used to spend what seemed like half a day making gingerbread cookies. The dough was temperamental, and it took hours to frost all the cookies. One glorious December day, I was invited to a cookie exchange party where someone brought these easy, moist, spice-laden wonders that I've been making every holiday season since discovering them.

Makes approximately 36 bars

2¾ cups all-purpose flour

1¼ teaspoons baking soda

1 teaspoon ground cinnamon

1 teaspoon ground ginger

1¼ cups butter, softened

1¼ cups packed light brown sugar

⅔ cup granulated sugar

3 large eggs

1 teaspoon vanilla extract

⅓ cup unsulfured molasses

1½ cups white chocolate chips

Preheat oven to 350°F. Coat a 17 x 12-inch rimmed baking sheet with cooking spray. Line the bottom with parchment cut to fit and coat parchment with spray.

Whisk together flour, baking soda, and spices. Set aside.

In a large bowl, beat butter and sugars on medium speed until pale and fluffy. Add eggs, one at a time, beating well after each addition. Mix in vanilla and molasses. Gradually add flour mixture and beat until just combined. Stir in white chocolate chips.

Spread batter in prepared pan. Bake for about 25 minutes, until edges are golden. Let cool completely on a wire rack. Cut into bars or use cookie cutters to cut out shapes. Store in an airtight container.

Tip: *Spray your measuring cup with nonstick spray before measuring the molasses and the sticky stuff will slide right out.*

Oatmeal Cookies

People who sneak raisins into cookies are the reason I have trust issues. You think you are biting into a chocolate chip and instead—a raisin! These oatmeal cookies are a fun twist on an old standard, without a raisin in sight. Delicious dried cranberries are accented with crunchy pecans and chunks of creamy white chocolate. Of all the cookies I bake, this one is the hardest to resist sneaking a pinch or two of batter right out of the bowl.

Makes approximately 36 cookies

¾ cup butter, softened

¾ firmly packed brown sugar

½ cup granulated sugar

2 eggs

1 teaspoon vanilla extract

1½ cups all-purpose flour

1 teaspoon baking soda

1½ teaspoons ground cinnamon

½ teaspoon salt

3 cups quick or old-fashioned oats

1 cup dried cranberries

½ cup chopped pecans

1½ cups white chocolate chunks (or chips)

Preheat oven to 350°F.

In a large bowl, beat butter and sugars on medium speed until creamy. Add eggs and vanilla; beat well.

In a medium bowl, mix flour, baking soda, cinnamon, salt, and oats. Add flour mixture to batter. Mix well, then stir in cranberries, pecans, and white chocolate.

Drop dough by rounded teaspoonfuls onto ungreased cookie sheets. Bake for 7 to 8 minutes, until barely brown.

Remove from oven and cool on wire rack. When completely cool, store tightly covered.

Sugar Cookies

I've always enjoyed baking, especially cookies. When I was in high school, I started experimenting with recipes. I soon found myself on a quest to create the best sugar cookie. It had to be soft and tender, light and flavorful. After many, many trials and errors, I came up with this recipe that never fails to deliver soft, delicious sugar cookies.

Makes approximately 48 cookies (depending on size of cookie cutters)

1 cup butter, softened

¾ cup granulated sugar

¼ cup powdered sugar

2 eggs

1 teaspoon vanilla extract

½ teaspoon lemon juice

1 teaspoon baking powder

1 teaspoon salt

2½ cups all-purpose flour

Frosting

Preheat oven to 375°F.

In a large bowl, beat butter with sugars and eggs until fluffy and light. Add vanilla extract and lemon juice.

In a separate bowl, mix baking powder, salt, and flour. Gradually add to dough until well mixed. Cover bowl with plastic wrap and refrigerate for at least an hour.

Sprinkle flour over a clean, dry surface, then roll out half the dough. Cut into desired shapes and place on an ungreased baking sheet. Roll out and repeat with the remaining dough. Bake for approximately 6 to 8 minutes, until dough is just set, but not brown.

Remove from oven and let cool in the pan for a minute, then transfer to a wire rack to cool. When completely cooled, frost and decorate.

Note: *Skip the need to roll and cut out cookies by pressing dough into a baking pan for easy and yummy bar cookies.*

Molasses Sugar Cookies

Amy Fenley of AJ Carriages shares this recipe her mother passed down to her. The cookies are full of flavor, and so soft. Absolutely delicious!

Makes approximately 30 cookies

¾ cup vegetable oil

1 cup granulated sugar

¼ cup molasses

1 egg

2 cups sifted all-purpose flour

2 teaspoons soda

½ teaspoon ground cloves

½ teaspoon ground ginger

1 teaspoon ground cinnamon

½ teaspoon salt

Preheat oven to 375°F.

Mix oil, sugar, molasses, and egg; beat well.

Sift together flour, soda, cloves, ginger, cinnamon, and salt; add to first mixture. Mix well and chill.

Form in 1-inch balls, roll in granulated sugar, and place 2 inches apart on an ungreased baking sheet. Bake for 8 to 10 minutes. Remove from oven and cool on a wire rack.

CAKES AND PIES

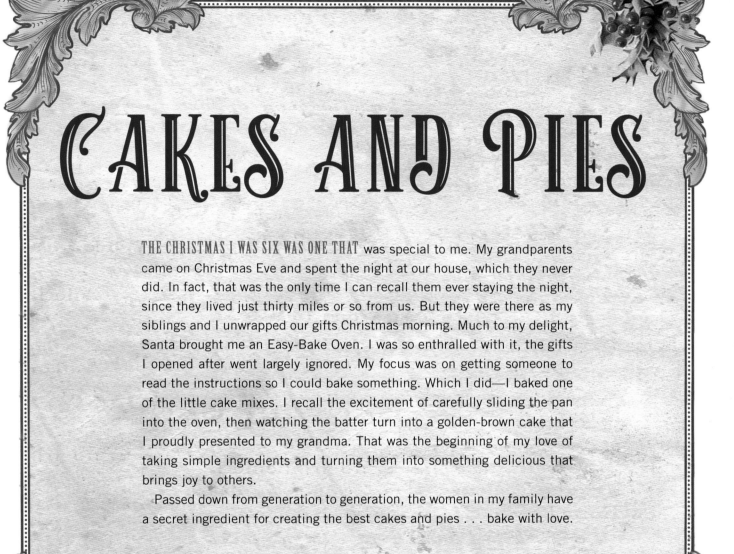

THE CHRISTMAS I WAS SIX WAS ONE THAT was special to me. My grandparents came on Christmas Eve and spent the night at our house, which they never did. In fact, that was the only time I can recall them ever staying the night, since they lived just thirty miles or so from us. But they were there as my siblings and I unwrapped our gifts Christmas morning. Much to my delight, Santa brought me an Easy-Bake Oven. I was so enthralled with it, the gifts I opened after went largely ignored. My focus was on getting someone to read the instructions so I could bake something. Which I did—I baked one of the little cake mixes. I recall the excitement of carefully sliding the pan into the oven, then watching the batter turn into a golden-brown cake that I proudly presented to my grandma. That was the beginning of my love of taking simple ingredients and turning them into something delicious that brings joy to others.

Passed down from generation to generation, the women in my family have a secret ingredient for creating the best cakes and pies . . . bake with love.

Chocolate Mint Bundt Cake

Captain Cavedweller's Grandma Nell loved to cook and bake. She collected hundreds of recipes and entered dozens of contests during her lifetime. One day when we were at her house, she served a moist, delicious bundt cake that was so, so good. I had to have the recipe and she willingly shared it. I blame her for my love of bundt cakes! They always turn out so well and are easy to take to potlucks and parties. This one features a mint-flavored cream cheese filling that pairs delightfully with the rich chocolate of the cake.

Makes 10–12 servings

CAKE

3 eggs

1 chocolate cake mix

1 small box instant chocolate pudding

½ cup oil

1 cup sour cream

½ cup water

½ cup chocolate chips

FILLING

1 (8-ounce) package cream cheese, softened

1 egg

1 teaspoon mint extract

½ cup granulated sugar

Green food coloring, optional

FROSTING

1½ cups semi-sweet chocolate chips

1 (14-ounce) can sweetened condensed milk

2 tablespoons butter, melted

Preheat oven to 350°F. Grease and flour a bundt cake pan and set aside.

In a large mixing bowl, lightly beat three eggs, until just broken up. Add cake mix, pudding, oil, sour cream, and water, mixing on medium-high speed for 2 minutes. Stir in ½ cup chocolate chips. Set aside.

Combine cream cheese, one egg, mint flavoring, and sugar, mixing on medium speed until well blended. If you want the filling to be green, add a few drops of green food coloring and stir until incorporated.

Spoon half the cake batter into the bundt pan. Add the cream cheese filling (but do not stir!). Top with remaining batter. If you are using a smaller bundt pan, there will be enough batter for two cakes.

Bake for 1 hour, until the edges of the cake begin to pull away from the pan. Remove from the oven and cool before inverting onto a cake plate.

In a microwave-safe bowl, combine chocolate chips, sweetened condensed milk, and butter. Microwave on high for 1 minute. Stir, then heat for another minute, in 30-second intervals, making sure chips are melted.

Drizzle frosting over cake (I like to pour it on thick!). You can garnish the cake with Andés Mints, crushed spearmint hard candy pieces, or sprigs of mint. For best flavor, bake the cake a day ahead of time and refrigerate until ready to serve.

Coconut Raspberry Cake

If you are a fan of coconut, you'll love this made-from-scratch cake, full of bold flavor and sweet raspberry filling! Whether you have a small family gathering or a large party to attend, this cake makes a beautiful addition to any holiday table.

Makes approximately 12 servings

CAKE

½ cup butter, softened

½ cup vegetable oil

1½ cups granulated sugar

2 teaspoons coconut extract

6 large egg whites, room temperature

1½ cups coconut milk

½ cup sour cream

3½ cups cake flour

4 teaspoons baking powder

½ teaspoon salt

FILLING

4 cups raspberries

⅓ cup granulated sugar

⅛ teaspoon salt

3 tablespoons water

3 tablespoons cornstarch

TOPPING

2 cups heavy whipping cream

½ cup powdered sugar

1 teaspoon coconut extract

2–3 cups sweetened flake coconut

1½ cups raspberries

Preheat oven to 350°F. Grease three 8-inch cake pans and line the bottoms with parchment paper. Set aside.

In a large mixing bowl, cream butter, oil, and sugar together until smooth. Beat in 2 teaspoons coconut extract and egg whites. Mix on medium-high speed for 2 minutes. Add coconut milk and sour cream, mixing until combined.

Mix in cake flour, baking powder, and salt.

Divide batter among the prepared pans. Bake for 25 to 30 minutes, until cake pulls away from edges of the pan or a toothpick inserted in the center comes out clean. Remove from oven and cool on wire racks.

To make the filling, combine raspberries, sugar, and salt in a saucepan over medium heat. Bring to a boil. Cook over medium heat for 5 minutes, stirring frequently, until berries break down. In a small bowl, combine cornstarch and water, whisking until smooth. Add cornstarch mixture to raspberry mixture, stirring constantly, and return to a boil. Cook a minute or two, until very thick, stirring constantly. Spoon mixture into a bowl; cover and refrigerate until ready to layer cake.

To make the topping, whip cream until light and fluffy. Add powdered sugar and coconut extract, mixing until blended.

After washing the raspberries to top the cake, drain on paper towels and gently pat dry.

Assemble the cake on a cake platter or plate. Between each layer spread the raspberry filling. If desired, you can also add a layer of whipped cream and coconut. Frost the cake with the whipped cream, then press coconut into the cream until cake is covered. Top with raspberries and refrigerate until ready to serve.

Tip: *If you don't have cake flour handy, for each cup you need, measure a cup of all-purpose flour into a bowl, remove two tablespoons, then add in two tablespoons of cornstarch. Stir to blend.*

North Pole Cake

Years ago, when Captain Cavedweller and I were newly wed, we hosted his family for a Christmas Eve celebration. His dad loves ice cream, so I found a recipe for a dessert that was frozen, featured ice cream, and, best of all, looked simple to make. Unfortunately, I didn't make sure the bottom was secure on the springform pan before I went to set it in the freezer. I picked up the pan and turned away from the counter as the bottom fell to the floor. A combination of cracker crust and runny, gooey filling splashed all over the kitchen. Impressively, it covered everything from the ceiling to the floor. Our dog, who had been keenly watching the proceedings, thought Santa had arrived early and eagerly dashed around the kitchen lapping up all the sweet goodness she could before she was chased outside.

Luckily, I had enough ingredients to start over, and the dessert turned out beautifully. Since then, I've made this dessert many times and it is always a hit. You can use any ice cream/pudding/crust combination you like, but my favorite is the one I share here.

Makes approximately 12 servings

CRUST

25 finely ground chocolate sandwich cookies

4 tablespoons butter, melted

FILLING

1 (8-ounce) package cream cheese, softened

1 large box instant vanilla pudding

2 cups milk

4 cups peppermint ice cream, softened

1 teaspoon mint extract

Mix cookie crumbs with butter and press into the bottom of a springform pan. Set aside.

In a large mixing bowl, blend cream cheese, pudding, and milk. When thoroughly combined, mix in the ice cream, then stir in extract. Pour filling on top of crust and freeze overnight or for several hours until firm.

Garnish with toppings of your choice just before serving.

Note: *Here are some additional flavor combination ideas:*

- *Vanilla pudding and butter toffee ice cream with golden sandwich cookies for the crust. Top with caramel sauce and bits of crushed toffee candy bars before serving.*

- *Chocolate pudding and turtle ice cream with a shortbread crust. Top with dollops of whipped cream and toasted pecans.*

- *Pumpkin pudding, vanilla ice cream, and a gingersnap crust. Garnish with dollops of whipped cream and sprinkles of cinnamon.*

Pumpkin Roll

My aunt Louise was a wonderful cook and just one of those sweet, caring people who never had anything bad to say about anyone. The first time I tasted her pumpkin roll, I was hooked, and she kindly shared the recipe. I've made it nearly every Christmas season, as the batter-speckled recipe card can attest. You can bake it with walnuts or pecans, although I generally leave mine nut free (due to a revolt of Captain Cavedweller's cousins the one year I added nuts!). The pumpkin roll is always amazingly good, and each bite brings fond memories of an auntie I greatly miss.

Makes approximately 10 servings

CAKE

3 eggs

1 cup granulated sugar

⅔ cup canned pumpkin

1 teaspoon lemon juice

¾ cup all-purpose flour

1 teaspoon baking powder

2 teaspoons ground cinnamon

1 teaspoon ground ginger

½ teaspoon ground nutmeg

1 cup finely chopped nuts, optional

FILLING

1 cup powdered sugar

1 (8-ounce) package cream cheese, softened

¼ cup butter, softened

1 teaspoon vanilla extract

¼ cup maraschino cherries, for garnish

Powdered sugar, for dusting

Preheat oven to 350°F. Grease and flour an 11 x 15-inch baking sheet.

Beat eggs on high speed for 5 minutes in a large mixing bowl until light and fluffy. Gradually beat in sugar. Stir in pumpkin and lemon juice.

In a small bowl, combine flour, baking powder, cinnamon, ginger, and nutmeg. Fold dry ingredients into pumpkin mixture.

Spread batter into prepared baking sheet. Sprinkle with nuts, if desired. Bake for 15 minutes, then remove from oven. Immediately invert cake onto a clean cotton tea towel liberally sprinkled with powdered sugar. Roll cake and towel up together, jelly roll style, starting from the short side. Cool completely.

Combine powdered sugar, cream cheese, butter, and vanilla on medium speed until smooth. Unroll cake and spread with filling. Reroll cake (without the towel), wrap in plastic wrap, and refrigerate until ready to serve.

Cut into 1-inch slices and garnish with cherries and a dusting of powdered sugar.

Vanilla Crumb Cake

"One of my favorite recipes that I enjoy making and know by heart now is actually one I learned in middle school in one of my home economics classes. Vanilla Crumb Cake tastes amazing with vanilla ice cream!" —Jessica Miller of Ranch Studio Artworks

Makes approximately 9 servings

1 cup all-purpose flour

¾ cup granulated sugar

1 teaspoon baking powder

¼ cup cold butter or margarine

1 egg

⅓ cup milk

½ teaspoon vanilla extract

Preheat oven to 375°F. Grease a 9 x 9-inch baking pan and set aside.

Sift together flour, sugar, and baking powder. With a pastry blender, mix butter into flour until crumbly. Measure out 1 cup of crumbs and set aside for the topping.

Mix the egg, milk, and vanilla with remaining crumb mixture. Beat until smooth. Pour batter into pan and sprinkle reserved dry crumbs evenly over the top.

Bake for 20 to 30 minutes.

Remove from oven and serve with vanilla ice cream.

Caramel Meringue Pie

The first time I made this pie, I wasn't sure what to expect. Captain Cavedweller, who is a bigger caramel fan than I am, was dubious when I handed him a slice. But then . . . one taste was all it took and we were fans! The smooth, rich custard is reminiscent of flan, only surrounded by a flaky crust and topped with fluffy meringue.

Makes approximately 8 servings

Baked pie crust (see recipe below)

Meringue (see recipe below)

½ cup granulated sugar

¼ cup cornstarch

2¼ cups half-and-half

⅓ cup dulce de leche

4 egg yolks (left over from meringue)

1 tablespoon butter

1 teaspoon vanilla extract

Prepare pie crust. Prepare meringue. Preheat oven to 325°F.

Stir together sugar and cornstarch in a heavy saucepan. Add half-and-half then dulce de leche. Cook over medium-high heat, stirring to blend ingredients, for 5 minutes, until thick and bubbly. Reduce heat to medium and cook 2 additional minutes while continuing to stir. Remove from heat.

Gradually combine 1 cup of the mixture into the egg yolks in a medium bowl, stirring to blend as you temper the eggs. Add egg mixture to saucepan ingredients and return to medium-high heat. Bring to a boil, stirring constantly. Reduce heat to medium and cook 2 more minutes, stirring constantly. Remove from heat, add butter and vanilla, and set aside.

Beat meringue for a few seconds to refresh.

Pour hot filling into the pastry shell, then immediately top with meringue, sealing to edge of the pastry. Using the back of a spoon, swirl meringue to make peaks, if desired.

Bake for 20 to 25 minutes, until meringue is golden brown. Remove from oven and cool on a wire rack for an hour. Chill at least 3 hours before serving.

Pie Crust

I've experimented with any number of pie crust recipes over the years, and this is one that has never let me down. The crust is always flaky and light.

Makes 2 (9-inch) pie crusts

2½ cups all-purpose flour

2 tablespoons sugar

¾ teaspoon salt

¾ cup cold butter, cut into small pieces

½ cup shortening

¼ cup vodka

¼ cup water

Preheat oven to 425°F.

In a bowl, stir together flour, sugar, and salt. Using a pastry blender, cut in butter and shortening until mixture is crumbly. Combine vodka and water and add 1 tablespoon at a time to flour mixture, using a fork to toss together. Continue adding liquid until dough comes together. Gently gather pastry into a ball and knead lightly. Wrap dough in plastic wrap and refrigerate for 30 minutes.

On a floured surface, divide dough in half. Slightly flatten one piece. (Freeze the other piece for another pie!) Roll to form a 12-inch-diameter circle. Carefully fold the pastry into fourths, then transfer to a pie plate. Unfold without stretching the dough. Trim to ½ inch beyond the edge of the plate. Fold under extra dough even with the pie plate's edge and form a decorative crust for a single-crust pie.

Prick bottom and sides of dough. Line with a double thickness of foil (or pie weights). Bake for 8 minutes. Remove foil and bake an additional 5 to 7 minutes, until golden brown. Cool on a wire rack.

MERINGUE

I used to avoid making meringue because I couldn't seem to get it quite right. Most often, the culprit was a weepy meringue, leaving liquid on top of the pie filling. This recipe fixes that problem. The keys to successful meringue are making it before the filling, beating the egg whites to the proper point, spreading meringue immediately onto the hot filling to seal it, and leaving the meringue in the oven until it's fully cooked.

Makes enough topping for 1 pie

4 eggs

2 teaspoons cornstarch

½ cup water

1 teaspoon vanilla extract

½ teaspoon cream of tartar

½ cup granulated sugar

Separate eggs, reserving the yolks for the Caramel Meringue Pie filling.

Place egg whites in a clean glass bowl and let stand until room temperature. Cold eggs tend to separate cleanly because the yolks are firmer. Egg whites at room temperature will quickly beat into a lovely foam, hence the reason to separate them while cold, then wait until warm before beating.

Mix cornstarch and water together in a microwave-safe cup. Heat for 30 seconds and stir. Heat an additional 30 seconds, or until boiling. Set aside. The addition of cornstarch to the meringue helps prevent shrinking and chases away those annoying droplets that can get into the pie filling.

Add vanilla and cream of tartar to egg whites. The cream of tartar helps egg whites expand and hold the foam structure.

Beat with a mixer on medium speed until soft peaks form. At the soft peak stage, egg whites will slide around in the bowl if it's tilted.

Add sugar 1 tablespoon at a time, beating on high. Add warm cornstarch mixture, a little at a time, until incorporated and stiff, glossy peaks form. At this point, if you hold up a beater, meringue should stand straight out on it.

CRUMBLY APPLE PIE

"This is my all-time favorite and most requested pie, but the recipe isn't mine. I randomly received it in the mail 25 years ago. It was part of a promotional packet. I make this pie at Christmas, Thanksgiving, and any time I need to say 'thank you' to someone in our community." —Carla Harrison, auctioneer and wife of rodeo barrelman John Harrison

Makes approximately 8 servings

CRUST

1 cup all-purpose flour

½ teaspoon salt

⅓ cup shortening, chilled

¼ cup ice water

FILLING

7 medium apples, peeled, cored, and thinly sliced

½ cup granulated sugar

1 teaspoon ground cinnamon

¼ teaspoon ground nutmeg

¼ teaspoon salt

TOPPING

¾ cup firmly packed dark brown sugar

¾ cup all-purpose flour

½ teaspoon ground nutmeg

⅓ cup cold butter, cut onto small pieces

Place oven rack in lowest position. Preheat oven to 400°F.

In a medium bowl, combine flour and salt. Using a pastry blender, cut shortening into flour mixture until coarse crumbs form. Add water, 1 tablespoon at a time, tossing with a fork, until a dough forms. Shape into a disk, wrap in plastic wrap, and chill for 30 minutes.

On a floured surface, using a floured rolling pin, roll dough into a 12-inch circle. Fit into a 9-inch pie pan. Trim excess dough, leaving a 1-inch overhang; make a decorative edge.

For the filling, mix together apples with sugar, cinnamon, nutmeg, and salt. Spoon into crust.

For the topping, mix together brown sugar, flour, and nutmeg. Using a pastry blender, cut butter into brown sugar mixture until coarse crumbs form. Sprinkle apples evenly with topping.

Bake for approximately 35 minutes, until topping is lightly browned and filling is bubbly. If pie is browning too quickly, cover loosely with aluminum foil. Transfer to a wire rack to cool.

Pear Cobbler

One year, as a gift for my mom, I asked my grandmas, aunts, and cousins to share their favorite recipes. I then transferred them all into a book for Mom, but kept copies of the recipes for myself, too! This cobbler recipe comes from my aunt Kathleen and is one of Captain Cavedweller's favorite desserts. You can make it with any type of fruit that is fresh and in season.

Makes approximately 10 servings

¼ cup butter

1 cup all-purpose flour

1 cup granulated sugar

2 tablespoons baking powder

⅔ cup milk

4 cups peeled, cored, and thinly sliced pears

1 teaspoon ground cinnamon

½ teaspoon ground nutmeg

Preheat oven to 325°F.

In a 9 x 13-inch baking dish, melt butter in oven.

Mix flour, sugar, baking powder, and milk until just combined. Pour over the top of the melted butter. Do not stir!

Toss pears with cinnamon and nutmeg. Add fruit on top of dough. Do not stir!

Bake for 1 hour. Remove from oven and let cool.

Serve with a generous topping of vanilla ice cream sprinkled with a dash of nutmeg.

Sour Cream Apple Pie

My dad loves pie. If you ask him what kind he prefers, he'll say "hot or cold." However, one of his absolute favorite pies is sour cream raisin. Since raisins and I aren't the best of friends, I decided to give this sour cream apple pie a try. Turns out, that was an entirely tasty decision. It comes Dad-approved!

Makes approximately 8 servings

1 unbaked pie crust

FILLING

2 tablespoons all-purpose flour

¼ teaspoon salt

¾ cup granulated sugar

¼ teaspoon ground nutmeg

1 egg

1 cup sour cream

1 teaspoon vanilla extract

3 cups peeled, cored, and thinly sliced apples

TOPPING

⅔ cup granulated sugar

⅔ cup all-purpose flour

2 teaspoons ground cinnamon

4 tablespoons cold butter, cut into small pieces

Preheat oven to 400°F.

Bake pie crust for 10 minutes, then remove from oven.

Prepare the filling while the pie crust bakes. Stir together flour, salt, sugar, and nutmeg in a bowl. Combine egg, sour cream, and vanilla in another bowl. Mix well. Add dry ingredients to egg mixture, stirring to blend well. Incorporate apples, then spoon mixture into the pie shell.

Bake for 15 minutes, then reduce temperature to 350°F and bake an additional 30 minutes.

For the topping, combine sugar, flour, and cinnamon in a bowl. Cut in butter until crumbly, using a pastry blender or fork.

Remove pie from oven and increase temperature to 400°F. Sprinkle crumb topping over pie. Return to oven and bake for 10 minutes. Remove and cool on a wire rack.

BLACK FOREST TRIFLE

Renee Moss shares this elegant dessert that's so easy to make. It's a treat the Moss family enjoys on Christmas as part of their traditions. Serve it at a special holiday gathering or as the finishing note for your Christmas dinner.

Makes approximately 12 servings

1 devil's food cake mix, and accompanying ingredients

2 Hershey's milk chocolate bars

1 (30-ounce) can cherry pie filling

1 teaspoon almond extract

½ cup cranberry-cherry juice

2 (3.3-ounce) packages white chocolate instant pudding

2 cups cold milk

1 container frozen whipped topping, thawed

Preheat oven to 350°F. Cut an 8½-inch square of parchment paper and place in the bottom of a square baking pan.

Prepare cake mix according to package directions; spread over bottom of pan. Bake for 25 minutes or until wooden pick inserted in center comes out clean. Cool completely.

Loosen cake from sides of pan and invert cake onto a cutting board. Remove parchment. Cut cake into 1-inch cubes using a bread knife; set aside. Chop one and a half of the chocolate bars into small pieces. Reserve remaining chocolate for garnishing.

Combine cherry pie filling and almond extract in a mixing bowl; remove ½ cup for garnishing and set aside. Stir juice into cherry pie filling.

In another large bowl, whisk pudding mixes with milk until mixture begins to thicken. Fold in whipped topping.

To assemble trifle, place half the cake cubes in the bottom of a trifle bowl or tall serving bowl. Layer half the cherry pie filling mixture evenly over cake cubes. Sprinkle with half the chopped chocolate and top with half the pudding mixture, pressing lightly. Repeat layers.

Garnish with reserved cherry pie filling and chocolate curls made with reserved chocolate. (Use a vegetable peeler to create curls.) Refrigerate at least 30 minutes before serving.

CANDY

ADMITTEDLY, I HAVE A SWEET TOOTH and come by it quite naturally (thanks, Dad!). Some of my all-time favorite treats are special traditional items we make only during the holidays. As I child, I remember watching my mom make divinity. She'd always check the weather first, because she said a cloudy day made a difference in how the candy turned out. My grandma made the best fudge, and Captain Cavedweller's grandmother made the most delicious peanut brittle.

If you're looking for a little something sweet to enjoy or share this holiday season, here are some of my favorites!

Chocolate Cheesecake Cherries

Inspired by delicious, sweet cherries, these cheesecake-filled bites dipped in chocolate are so good it will be hard to stop at just one!

Makes 60 cherries

60 fresh sweet cherries

2 ounces spreadable cream cheese

2 tablespoons powdered sugar

1 teaspoon vanilla extract

3 tablespoons whipped cream

12 ounces chocolate candy melts

Wash and dry cherries. Pit cherries, placing on paper towels to dry.

Combine cream cheese, powdered sugar, and vanilla. Stir in whipped cream and spoon mixture into a piping bag with a tip that will fit inside the hole of the pitted cherry. Squirt filling into the cherry.

In a small microwave-safe, resealable bag, melt about 1 ounce of chocolate candy melts, then spread it on the cherry to cover the hole. Place in the freezer for about 5 minutes.

Measure about a third of the remaining chocolate candy melts in a microwave-safe bowl and melt according to package directions. Dip each cherry into the melted chocolate, turning to coat. Allow excess to drip off and place cherries on a parchment paper–lined pan. Working with the candy melt in three batches keeps the chocolate from setting up too quickly.

Cool at room temperature for about 20 minutes, then refrigerate until ready to serve.

Chocolate Snowflakes and Trees

Place chocolate snowflakes and trees in small cellophane bags for gift-giving, or use them to top cupcakes, cookies, or float in a cup of hot chocolate for a bit of added festive fun.

Makes approximately 40 pieces

1 cup white chocolate candy melts

1 cup milk chocolate candy melts

Candy sprinkles, optional

Fit two pastry bags with writing tips.

Line a large baking sheet with parchment.

In a microwave-safe bowl, melt the white chocolate candy according to package directions. Fill one pastry bag with the melted candy and pipe snowflake shapes. Melt the milk chocolate candy for the second pastry bag and pipe trees. You can top with sprinkles or edible glitter for added panache.

CREAM CHEESE MINTS

The first time I had these mints was when Captain Cavedweller's grandmother asked a friend to make them for our wedding reception. Being the sappy girl that I am, I still have one preserved mint. The mints are easy to make and so delicious, with a fresh burst of mint flavor.

Makes 16–20 servings

1 (8-ounce) package cream cheese, softened

2 tablespoons butter, softened

1 teaspoon peppermint extract

7 cups powdered sugar

3–4 drops food coloring, optional

Beat cream cheese and butter in a mixing bowl until smooth. Add peppermint extract and mix well. Add 1 cup of the powdered sugar. When blended, add remaining powdered sugar, beating until smooth. Mix in food coloring, if using.

Press into candy molds (silicone work best) or transfer to a pastry bag with a large tip (a star works well). Pipe onto a parchment paper–lined baking sheet. Let rest on the counter for 1 hour, then place in the freezer to harden. Keep chilled.

Nut Goodie Bars

The first time I tasted this delicious chocolate confection was when my wonderful auntie made them for a holiday gathering. Being a chocolate devotee even as a child, I was captivated by the flavors. Once I was old enough to make them myself, Aunt Robbie gladly shared the recipe, and I am pleased to share it with you today. These are always a hit, so quick and easy to make, and so yummy. Although some may refer to these as "Rocky Road Bars," I call them by the name my aunt gave them.

Makes approximately 24 bars

1 bag semi-sweet chocolate chips

1 bag butterscotch chips

1 bag peanut butter chips

1 large bag mini marshmallows

1 small can (about 1½ cups) cocktail peanuts

Grease a 9 x 13-inch casserole dish and set aside.

In a large microwave-safe bowl, mix chips. Microwave for 45 seconds and then stir. Continue heating in 30-second intervals, stirring in between, until chips are melted. Stir well to blend. Mix in marshmallows and peanuts and then spread in casserole dish.

Let cool and cut into bars. These can be frozen for up to 4 weeks if kept in an airtight container.

TOFFEE

For years, I tried to make toffee, but something was always wrong. It was chewy. It had a weird burned flavor. It never set up. Then I happened upon a toffee recipe that only had four ingredients and sounded so simple. It was! By far, it is our family's favorite toffee of any we've had.

Makes approximately 12 servings

1 cup chopped pecans

1 cup semi-sweet chocolate chips

1 cup butter

2 cups brown sugar

Line a 9 x 13-inch baking sheet with parchment. Spray with nonstick cooking spray. Sprinkle nuts and chocolate chips evenly on the baking sheet. Set aside.

Melt the butter in a heavy saucepan on medium heat. Add the sugar, stirring constantly. Bring the mixture to a boil and boil for 7 minutes, continuing to stir.

Pour toffee over chips and nuts, spreading as needed. Let baking sheet rest on a kitchen towel on the counter for 30 minutes, then place in the freezer for at least 30 minutes to cure. Flip the pan over on a cutting board, remove parchment, then break toffee into pieces and serve.

GIFTS FROM THE KITCHEN

THERE'S NOTHING LIKE A GIFT YOU MADE YOURSELF to let people know you care, and a little lovin' from your kitchen is extra special. Homemade gifts for sharing (and eating!) don't have to take a lot of time, but they can be a lot of fun! And don't forget to make those gifts look festive, too. Tuck them into boxes or tins, or cute little cellophane bags tied with cheerful ribbon. The recipients will love the gift and the effort you went to in creating something unique and scrumptious just for them.

CHOCOLATE CHEX TREES

These yummy and adorable trees are so simple to make and a great project if you have kids at home who need something to do. Set the trees on a disposable plate, foil-wrapped piece of cardboard, or a large sugar cookie wrapped in cellophane for gift-giving!

Makes 6 trees

½ cup peanut butter

¼ cup Nutella

3 tablespoons butter, softened

1 cup powdered sugar

6 pretzel sticks (the thick kind, made for dipping)

3 cups Chocolate Chex cereal

Combine the peanut butter, Nutella, butter, and powdered sugar in a bowl.

On whatever you plan to use for a base, mold the peanut butter mixture around the pretzel stick until it stands upright and forms a slight cone shape.

Hold it steady by using the tip of the pretzel as a handle and begin inserting pieces of cereal into the peanut butter mixture in a symmetrical pattern around the pretzel stick. You can tip the cereal pieces up or down, depending on your personal preference. Add more cereal pieces, staggering them as you move upward, until you get near the top. Use broken pieces or cut them in half to get the smaller scale of branches near the top.

Place two pieces of cereal back to back to form the top.

Dust with powdered sugar.

Chocolate Raspberry Jam

Years ago, my mom found a recipe for chocolate raspberry jam. We all loved chocolate and raspberries, but we had no idea how much we'd love this delicious spread! Oh, my goodness. I think every drop was scraped out of each jar. Give this as a gift and be prepared for the grateful smiles that come your way. Add a little holiday flair to your jars by padding the tops with a bit of cotton batting and a piece of holiday fabric.

Makes approximately 8 jars

5 cups prepared raspberries (approximately 2 quarts fully ripe berries)

1 box Sure-Jell fruit pectin

5 ounces Baker's unsweetened chocolate, coarsely chopped

½ teaspoon butter

7 cups granulated sugar, measured into a separate bowl

Prepare boiling water canner. Heat clean jars in simmering water until ready for use. Do not boil. Wash lids and jar bands in warm soapy water. Set aside bands. Place lids in a saucepan, then pour boiling water over the top and let stand in hot water until ready to use.

Crush raspberries thoroughly. (Press pulp through a sieve to remove seeds if desired.) Measure exactly 5 cups of crushed fruit into a large saucepan.

Stir pectin into prepared fruit. Add chocolate and mix well. Add butter to reduce foaming. Bring mixture to a rolling boil (one that doesn't stop boiling when stirred) on high heat, stirring constantly. Stir in sugar. Return to full rolling boil and boil 1 minute, continuing to stir constantly. Remove from heat. Skim off foam with a metal spoon.

Immediately ladle into jars, filling to within ¼ inch of top. Wipe jar rims and threads with a clean cloth. Cover with lids. Screw bands on tightly.

Place jars on the elevated rack in canner. Lower rack into canner. Water must cover jars by an inch or two; add more boiling water if needed. Cover and bring water to a gentle boil. Process for 10 minutes, then remove jars and place upright on a towel to cool completely.

After jars cool, check seals by pressing the center of the lids with index finger. If lids spring back, lids are not sealed and refrigeration is necessary.

Elf Snack Mix

The first time I tasted this completely addicting treat was when our neighbor brought over a box of it as a gift. The combination of sweet and salty is so perfect. It's hard to stop with just one or two bites. Make extra so you have plenty for munching *and* giving away!

Makes 8 servings

10 cups popped popcorn

1 cup cocktail peanuts

2 cups pretzels

1 bag red and green M&Ms

1 package white chocolate candy melts

¼ cup Christmas sprinkles, optional

Combine popcorn, peanuts, pretzels, and M&Ms. Set aside.

Melt white chocolate candy according to package directions and pour over popcorn mixture. Stir well to coat. Top with Christmas sprinkles, if desired.

Store in an airtight container to keep fresh.

Peppermint Bowls

What could be better than giving a gift in an edible container? These cute peppermint bowls are easy to make and take hardly any time at all. Enjoy bringing people joy with this sweet gift!

Makes 1 bowl

19 hard peppermint candies

Preheat oven to 300°F. Place a silicone baking liner or parchment paper on a baking sheet (if using parchment paper, give it a light shot of nonstick cooking spray). Find a small glass bowl to use as a form; turn it upside down and lightly spray the outside with non-stick cooking spray.

Place one mint in the center of the baking sheet. Add six mints in a circle around the center, making sure mints touch and are as close as possible. Make another circle around the center with the remaining mints.

Slide the baking sheet into the oven. Ovens vary widely, but melting should take 6 to 8 minutes. Keep an eye on the candy. When the discs begin to shine and spread out, take them out and let rest for 20 seconds. They will harden quickly, so don't take more time than that.

The candy will be superhot, so grab your oven mitts and flip the silicone liner or parchment paper onto the bowl, centering it as best you can. Quickly press down the sides of the candy to mold around the bowl. Leave the candy on the bowl for about 5 minutes, until fully set, then gently twist it off. Fill with treats.

Popcorn Cake

It was October, just a month after I'd arrived at college nine hours away from everything and everyone I'd always known. My birthday was fast approaching and I was thoroughly homesick, wanting to be back at the farm and out of the city. Then a box of surprises arrived from my parents, including a wonderful, sticky, messy cake that made me feel loved and not quite so desperate to get back home. I've made this popcorn cake many, many times through the years, but I don't think any of them have tasted quite as good as the first one Mom sent in a box filled with love.

Makes 8 servings

½ cup oil

½ cup butter

1 large bag mini marshmallows

24 cups popped popcorn

1½ cups peanuts

1 cup spiced gumdrops

Mix oil, butter, and marshmallows in a large bowl. Microwave at 20- to 30-second increments, stirring between each set until marshmallows are melted and oil and butter are mixed in nicely. (It will still look a little oily.)

Mix in popped popcorn, peanuts, and gumdrops. Press into a greased bundt or angel food cake pan. Leave at room temperature for an hour or so until cake is set, then tip upside down to remove from pan.

Serve immediately, or wrap in cellophane for gift-giving.

Ranch Crackers

If you have someone among your circle of family and friends who loves savory flavors, especially ranch, they will adore these crackers—and you. So simple to make, and so hard to stop eating at just one, or four, or was that a dozen?

Makes 80–100 crackers

1 box buttery round crackers, such as Ritz

½ cup butter

1 packet ranch seasoning mix

½ cup shredded Parmesan cheese

Preheat oven to 300°F. Line two large baking sheets with parchment paper.

In a large bowl, melt the butter and mix in the entire packet of ranch seasoning mix. Add crackers to the bowl and gently toss to coat.

Place crackers on the baking sheets in a single layer and sprinkle with cheese. Bake for 15 minutes.

Note: *If you want to give the crackers a little kick, add crushed red pepper flakes to the ranch seasoning mix.*

SPICE RUBS

Spice rubs are so simple to mix together, and make such a great present for your meat-loving friends. Mix and spoon into little tins, then attach a label for a wonderful, aromatic gift!

Each recipe makes ½–1 cup

BBQ SPICE RUB

½ cup brown sugar

½ cup paprika

1 tablespoon black pepper

1 tablespoon salt

1 tablespoon chili powder

1 tablespoon onion powder

STEAK SPICE RUB

2 tablespoons black pepper

2 tablespoons coarse sea salt

2 tablespoons paprika

1 tablespoon crushed coriander seeds

1 tablespoon garlic powder

1 tablespoon onion powder

HOT SPICE RUB

2 tablespoons salt

2 tablespoons garlic powder

1 tablespoon black pepper

1 tablespoon red pepper flakes

2 tablespoons cayenne pepper

2 tablespoons Hungarian paprika

2 tablespoons chili powder

2 tablespoons onion powder

1 tablespoon dry mustard

2 tablespoons brown sugar

These recipes couldn't be simpler. Choose your rub flavor, mix ingredients together, and store in an air-tight container.

RESOURCES

Here are some helpful hints on where to find some of the little things to make your Cowboy Christmas memorable.

DECK THE HALLS:

Weather can wreak havoc on your beautifully installed outdoor lights. Twist and Seal makes boxes that snap over the connecting plugs on your string lights and are made specifically to help protect the connections from water and weather: twistandseal.com

If your ornaments are heirlooms, you'll want to protect those memories in a high-quality storage box. I recommend the archival quality boxes from Ultimate Christmas: ultimate christmas.com.

WRAPPED IN LOVE:

My go-to places to find high-quality wrapping paper are Hallmark stores, Marshalls, and Acorn Spring Ranch. Also, use tape meant for wrapping gifts, like Scotch Satin GiftWrap Tape, for the best results.

Two of my favorite places for essential oils and aromatherapy are Bath & Body Works and DōTERRA. Etsy is a great place to find a variety of unique aprons.

If you are looking for quality candles, Yankee Candle and Greenleaf are among my favorites.

HOME FOR THE HOLIDAYS:

The best solvent I've found for cleaning up red wine stains on fabric is Wine Away: wineaway .com.

PRESERVING MEMORIES:

Personalized photo gifts are so accessible in the digital age. Here are a few sources for some cool and memorable gifts using your own images:

- **Shutterfly**—From iPhone cases to personalized lunch bags, you can personalize so many things through this site. One of my favorite things to order are the photo books. You can use the templates or create your own designs. I've given these books as gifts after weddings, for birthdays, and for anniversaries: shutterfly.com.

- **Snapfish**—You'll find everything from photo keychains to customized playing cards at this website: snapfish.com.

- **Mpix**—From calendars and magnets to metal dog tags, this site has an assortment of choices for turning your images into special gifts: mpix.com.

MADE FROM THE HEART:

Whether you're looking for someone to create a large, statement-worthy project or a small, intricate piece, Jessica and Derek at Ranch Studio artworks are up to the challenge. When I needed five hundred giveaways for an event, I sent a rough idea to Jessica. She worked with me to refine the idea and come up with exactly what I wanted—a leather bookmark. And all five hundred of them were perfectly crafted. She also didn't hesitate a second when I asked her to custom design a watch for me: ranchstudioartworks.com.

Silver spoons and china plates are treasured antiques. Special pieces can be upcycled into jewelry and other decorative items after their useful lives are at an end. Two great resources are The Recycled Spoon (therecycledspoon.com) and Vintage Revival (vintagerevival.com).

SHARE THE JOY:

For more information about Casey Colletti and Kacee Willbanks Colletti, and inspiration for your giving this season, visit their websites:

kaceewillbanksllc.com

fameandkane.com

youtube.com/user/kaceewillbanks

If you have trouble finding a place to volunteer, look at online resources like Volunteer Match: volunteermatch.org.

APPETIZERS AND BEVERAGES:

You can find sugar rimmer crystals at liquor stores, or at restaurant supplies stores like webstaurantstore.com.

INDEX

R

S

About the Author

A hopeless romantic with a bit of sarcasm thrown in for good measure, **Shanna Hatfield** is a *USA Today* best-selling author of sweet romantic fiction written with a healthy dose of humor. In addition to blogging and eating too much chocolate, this former farm girl is completely smitten with her husband, lovingly known as Captain Cavedweller.

Shanna creates character-driven romances with realistic heroes and heroines. Her historical Westerns have been described as "reminiscent of the era captured by *Bonanza* and *The Virginian*," while her contemporary works have been called "laugh-out-loud funny, and a little heart-pumping sexy without being explicit in any way."

A lifelong fan of rodeo, Shanna contributes a portion of her book sales to the Justin Cowboy Crisis Fund during the holiday season.